Body Projects in Japanese Childcare

Body Projects in Japanese Childcare

Culture, Organization and
Emotions in a Preschool

Eyal Ben-Ari

CURZON

First published in 1997
by Curzon Press
St John's Studios, Church Road, Richmond
Surrey, TW9 2QA

© 1997 Eyal Ben-Ari

Typeset in Garamond by LaserScript, Mitcham, Surrey
Printed in Great Britain by
TJ Press (Padstow) Ltd, Padstow, Cornwall

Chapter 3 was previously published in *Ethos* 24(1), 1996. Permission to
reprint was kindly given by the Psychological Section of the American
Anthropological Association.

British Library Cataloguing in Publication Data
A catalogue record for this book is available from the British Library

ISBN 0–7007–0448–5

*This book is dedicated to my father
and the memory of my mother*

Contents

Acknowledgements

My first debt is to the children and the staff of Katsura Day-Care Center. These people accepted and shared their lives with me. The center's director – Nakae-sensei – always proved patient and helpful. The center's head teacher – Yuko Yoshimura – was especially kind and has since also become a good friend.

This book was written during a sabbatical leave spent at The Department of Japanese Studies of the National University of Singapore, and later at The Department of Sociology and Anthropology of the Hebrew University. I am grateful to my colleagues and the administrative staff at these departments for providing very congenial and supportive conditions in which to work.

Earlier versions of some chapters were presented at a variety of seminars at the Department of Sociology and Anthropology of the Hebrew University, the Department of Sociology and Anthropology of Bar-Ilan University, the Department of Educational Policy at the University of Wisconsin, Madison, the Japanese Studies Centre of School of Oriental and African Studies, the Department of Japanese Studies at the National University of Singapore, and at a meeting of the European Association of Japanese Studies in Berlin. I would like to thank participants at these seminars for comments, and especially Efrat Ben-Ze'ev, Sarit Helman, Ilana Litwin, Pamela Lubell, Chihiro Thomson, and Timothy Tsu for their detailed suggestions. I would especially like to thank Susan Sared for her insights and support. Chapter 3 was originally presented at a workshop on 'Transformations in Contemporary East Asia' held to honor the retirement of Professors Zvi Schiffrin and Al Altman of the Hebrew University.

Financial assistance for this project was kindly provided by the Harry S. Truman Research Institute of the Hebrew University of Jerusalem, and the Otsuki Peace Fund of the Japan Friends of Israel (Kyoto).

My two sons' experience in various day-care centers in Israel, England and Japan spurred me towards this research project and always kept me wondering about the special magic of growing up. Throughout my work I have had a constant partner for support, discussion and the exchange of ideas: thank you, Edna.

A Note on Language

All Japanese words are romanized according to the modified Hepburn system. Long vowels, however, are rendered as a double letter rather than with a superscript bar.

People's names are given in the Japanese order with the personal name following the patronym. Names of prefectures, cities, and references have been rendered without long vowels.

Chapter 1

Introduction

This book examines the place of body practices and the management of emotions in Japanese preschools. I proceed from the
following, rather simple, proposition: while a host of very good
studies of Japanese preschools have been published in the past
decade, these works tend to overlook a number of key issues
related to embodiment and to affects. Borrowing from Featherstone
(1991; also Fruhestueck 1994), I propose to explore early childhood socialization as a set of 'body projects': a series of practices
undertaken (over time) to design the body according to prevailing
cultural definitions and images. The concept 'body projects' allows
us to understand how the body is, at one and the same time, a
malleable material good capable of being fashioned in a certain
manner, an entity which represents social relations and notions,
and an embodiment of affective attitudes and stances towards the
world. To be sure, body projects can be seen as individual undertakings in which people intentionally fashion their physical frame
to conform to accepted social notions. But the intriguing question
in regard to such projects in preschools involves the organizational
schemes that use the body in enculturating children. The analytical
challenge then, is to uncover the procedures and methods utilized
by such institutions to fashion children's physical forms and emotional postures and attitudes.

This volume tackles this set of themes by examining one institution of early childhood education: Katsura *Hoikuen* (Day-Care
Center). Based on fieldwork carried out in the summer of 1988 and
(for a short while) in the fall of 1994, my perspective is basically

ethnographic in its approach. In order to situate my study in relation to contemporary scholarship of the 'body' and of Japanese preschools, and in order to clearly identify the issues I have singled out for analysis, let me answer three questions in the framework of this introduction: why the focus on body practices and emotions? Why day-care centers? And why the specific case I have chosen to study?

From Cognition to Embodiment

There have been two waves of post-war research by Western scholars on childhood socialization in Japan. The first wave of studies which was published in the 1950s and 1960s focused on the family and the home. These studies dealt with such issues as motivation (De Vos 1973; 1986), personality (Lanham 1966; 1986), or infant–mother relations (Caudill and Weinstein 1969; Caudill and Plath 1986). Most (but not all) of these studies appear to have been grounded in one or a combination of two 'grand' approaches: the 'culture and personality' school as evinced in Benedict's (1946) classic volume and various versions of modernization theory (De Vos 1973; Vogel 1963).

The second wave of studies, which began during the late 1970s, continued to concentrate on families (for instance, Hess *et al.* 1980; Conroy *et al.* 1980; Fuller *et al.* 1986; Tanaka 1984), but added a new interest in preschools, in *institutions* of early childhood education. The rationale underlying these later studies was empirical and theoretical. On the one hand, scholars directed their attention to the extent and prevalence of such institutions. With about 95 per cent of children who enter first grade having attended kindergartens (*yoochien*) or day-care centers (*hoikuen*) (Tobin *et al.* 1989: 70) preschool is now nearly a universal experience for Japanese youngsters. On the other hand, the focus on preschools grew out of a recognition that as the exposure to formal education in preschool was a formative experience influencing children's later schooling, an examination of this experience would provide insights into how Japanese people gain abilities to carry out various social roles throughout their lives (Rohlen 1989a; 1989b).

Along these lines, in the past decade or so, a host of excellent studies of preschool education in Japan had been published. These studies include overviews like Hendry's (1986a) book or Boocock's (1989) article as well as examinations of specific institutions (Peak

1991a; Sano 1989; Tobin, Wu and Davidson 1989). In addition, other scholars have examined more specific issues such as pre-school curriculum, relations between teachers and mothers, peer control and the inculcation of individual responsibility and cross-cultural differences in notions of childcare (DeCoker 1989; Fujita 1989; Fujita and Sano 1988; Lewis 1989; Peak 1991b). These discussions have done much to further our understanding of the dynamics of custody and instruction in kindergartens and day-care centers.

At the base of the various studies of preschools which have been published during the 1980s and 1990s stand two kinds of models each of which belongs to a somewhat different intellectual tradition. The first, or cognitive model is found in the work of such scholars as Bachnik (1992; 1994), Rosenberger (1992) and Tobin (1992). The focus in this model is on the culture-specific definitions of self as found in Japan (Kelly 1991). As a consequence of this focus in examining socialization, advocates of this model either explore how children come to master certain basic cultural notions (such as the *uchi/soto* distinction), or reveal the ethno-classifications which underlie the care and instruction given to children (cf. White and Levine 1986; Kojima 1986). The advances made within this approach have been in the systematic presentation of the basic cognitive categories by which the Japanese self is defined.

The second model is a sophisticated version of an educational or learning model. It has been formulated in the work of such scholars as Peak (1989; 1991a), Shields (1989), DeCoker (1989) and foremostly Lewis (1987; 1991). Here the emphases are primarily on the relationships between teachers and pupils; the preparation of children for school life (and other social roles); and the inculcation of certain basic routines and habits. The contributions of this approach have been both to provide sound ethnographic depictions of pre-schools, and to underscore the role of caretakers in teaching children fundamental school related abilities (such as the capacities to concentrate or to be orderly in personal habits).

While both models have made considerable contributions to our understanding of Japanese preschools, they are seriously limited in terms of addressing issues of embodiment. Thus while there have been occasional openings in regard to other aspects of Japanese society (Kondo 1990; 1992; McVeigh 1993; 1994), as yet little has been done within both approaches to address the question of how body practices and the management of emotions enter the complex set of processes we term socialization. But this question is critical for understanding what happens during childhood. Take Berger and Luckmann's (1967; 203) proposition that socialization does not simply involve the intrinsic problems of learning, because

> the child resists the imposition of the temporal structure of society on the natural temporality of his organism. He resists eating and sleeping by the clock rather than by the biologically given demands of the organism.

From our point of view, the import of Berger and Luckmann's contention is not only that some children resist patterns imposed on them by caretakers (and parents), but that from the teachers' point of view these children become 'organizational problems'. The administration of naptimes and mealtimes, to put this by way of their example, is thus saturated with issues of power, physiological needs and demands, and cultural definitions of proper demeanor and behavior. The situation in which issues related to the body and to emotions have not been systematically integrated into the examination of Japanese preschools is all the more surprising given the growing social scientific attention to embodiment (Csordas 1993). Let me very briefly describe some of the features of this scholarly interest and then indicate the kinds of questions that it raises about early childhood education in Japan.

In general, the move towards 'the body' grew against the background of a wider dissatisfaction with the grand theories of the post-War social sciences: the 'modernization' and the 'culture and personality' schools. While the former dealt with roles and statuses defined in ideal terms, the latter considered configurations of personality type induced by cultural socialization. Both approaches, however, "fell foul of the difficulties implicit in dealing with the questions of deviance and change" (Strathern 1994: 43). At first the discontent with these approaches led to an appreciation of the dynamic processes – the negotiations, inventions and contestations – by which cultures are constructed. Then, a study of 'the person' began to be seen as offering the possibility of drawing on both of the older grand traditions without taking on their less tenable propositions: distinguishing between self and the person enabled a rerun of the older distinction between the individual and his or her social role to be incorporated into new debates. In the newer approach, "the focus has been cultural: self and person are seen as culturally defined concepts. Sociality enters when the negotiation of transactions between selves and persons is taken into account" (Strathern 1994: 43–4).

More recently, the discontentment with older approaches has led away from a mentalistic or cognitive model of social life and the focus on the 'person' has been combined with a wider move towards studying the body. While lack of space precludes a more ordered overview, it seems that interest in the body is the outcome of both social and theoretical developments; specifically, changes in the meaning of the body in contemporary post-industrial societies (Martin 1992). The main theoretical developments have been a gradual shift away from simple mind/body dichotomies and the reconceptualization of the mind/body relationship in a more holistic manner[1] (Lutz 1985; 1987); the incorporation of Pierre Bourdieu's (1977) ideas about *habitus* as propensities or inclinations which are beyond the grasp of consciousness into social scientific thought; and the influence of Michel Foucault's (1979; 1980) propositions about discipline and body/power on current studies. As a consequence of these developments 'conventional' issues such as childhood socialization are beginning to be examined in a new light. In this volume, I propose to examine and to offer a new approach to three issues which emerge out of the recent development in the scholarly study of embodiment.

Culture and motivation. The first issue is related to the limitation of the cognitive model in studies of early childhood socialization. Specifically, it is associated with the link between cognition, emotion and motivation. As I mentioned, a number of recent studies have illuminated the 'folk-' or 'ethno-theories' of childhood and childcare in Japan (White and Levine 1986; Tobin 1992). Such essays should be seen as part of a much broader move towards uncovering the basic cognitive categories or classifications that underlie what may be termed the Japanese world-view (Bachnik 1994; Rosenberger 1992). But if we are to gain a full understanding of socialization, we must not be content with sketching the main cultural definitions or schemas of child socialization that underlie the care given to youngsters in Japan. The trouble is that without an account of the relations between culture and motivation we may have an intuitive sense that there are culturally based strivings but we have no explanation for how these strivings are internalized and then govern behavior in subsequent situations (D'Andrade 1992: 23). As Strauss (1992: 10) notes, "motivation is not automatically acquired when cultural descriptions of reality are learned". Thus the problem is to show *how* cultural definitions gain 'directive', or motivational force.

Specifically, I contend that the assumption in most recent works about Japanese preschools is that the practices and educational forms found in these institutions somehow "naturally" lead to the inculcation of such cultural emphases as group orientedness or personal discipline. In many previous studies, preschool activities are treated as a sort of 'black box' through which the children move only to emerge properly socialized. What I do in this volume is to open up this 'black box' and to explore the interpersonal dynamics and individual centered experiences by which the children internalize the cultural definitions. My aim is to examine the manner by which educational goals and practices (many of which have been illuminated in previous studies) acquire motivational significance for the children. I suggest that this motivational significance is achieved via a link between official educational aims and both the bodily needs and demands of the children and their emotional stances toward others.

The dual nature of body practices. The second issue involves a limit of the educational model in studies of Japanese preschools. It centers on making problematical what we mean by the place of body practices in the internalization of cultural constructs. A reading of recent studies reveals that there are two analytically distinct dimensions involved in the manner – the actual mechanisms – by which children learn to embody culture. The first is the method by which certain practices gain strong motivational significance. The second, however, is the way in which preschool practices lead to educational goals becoming natural, habitual parts of the children's lives. Thus although the matter is not always clear, studies of the body and of emotions tend to lead in one of two directions: either the accent is on the coupling of cultural meanings to motivation via a set of positive reinforcements and more negative controls; or the stress (a la Bourdieu) is on propensities and implicit habits carried in one's comportment.

My contention is that while promoters of the educational model have been well aware of the importance of habits and the in-culcation of propensities, they have done little to place these issues in an explicit theoretical framework. Along these lines, my second aim is to differentiate and then to integrate (within the 'black box' of preschool) the more 'passive' mode of gradually learning to embody certain taken for granted habits and the more 'active' connection of such habits and practices to a set of incentives and inducements.

The body and resistances. The third issue is related to something that has hardly been touched upon either in the general literature on embodiment or in specific studies of Japanese preschools: the resistances that children mount in and around body processes and the emotional commitment and involvement demanded of them in preschools. These protests and oppositions are expressed in direct denials of teachers' requests and directives, but (given the power of caretakers over them) they are also expressed through a variety of obscenities, jokes, and general mischief that form an essential part of any child's life. The range of such behaviors all contain a potential for children to assume a critical stance towards preschool and towards what is being done to them.

The reason for examining these kinds of critical play are twofold. Empirically they help us appreciate the variety and the complexity of the experience of early childhood education in Japan. Theoretically, an analysis of such playful behavior raises questions about our conceptualization of (Japanese) children and just what it is that goes on in such institutions. If we accept the basic independent capacities of children then we begin to see them not as dependent and needing to be socialized, but as independent actors who participate in their own socialization and who can take an autonomous stance *vis-à-vis* teachers, other people and themselves.

Why Study Day-Care Centers?

Primarily as a result of the entry of women into the labor force (Hayashi 1985; Yamagata 1986; Carney and O'Kelly 1990) a substantial part of primary socialization in Japan takes place within preschools. In Japan, institutions of early childhood education are differentiated into *yoochien* (kindergartens) and *hoikuen* (day-care centers). Kindergartens are usually open half-days and cater for children aged four and five. Day-care centers normally operate for a whole day (often from seven in the morning until six at night) and cater to children of working mothers between the ages of a few months and six (in reality most of the children attend only after the age of two). In addition, while kindergartens fall under the jurisdiction of the Ministry of Education, day-care centers are run under the aegis of the Ministry of Health and Welfare.

In the past two decades, however, the type of institution which has shown the greatest rate of growth has been the day-care center. Today there are 22,000 public or publicly recognized day-care centers that cater to over 2 million children (Koseisho 1993; Tochio 1986: 3). At the point of entry into schools – that is, entry into primary school – about 30 per cent of children have attended day-care centers (Fujita 1989: 77). But as Tobin and his associates (1989: 209) state, with the falling birthrate "some Japanese pre-schools will have to close, and a gradual shift in women's life-styles from full-time mothering toward a more job- or career-centered orientation seems to favor survival of *hoikuen* over *yoochien* in the long run". Thus the grounds for studying day-care centers are primarily that these institutions are becoming more important in 'designing' the face of Japan's future generations: both in terms of preparing them for the Japanese educational system and (later) for entry into the work force.

But the justification for studying day-care centers also has to do with their organizational features. Many studies of Japanese pre-schools – like Tobin *et al.* (1989) or Hendry (1986a: 125) – have tended to examine institutions of early childhood education without differentiating between the special characteristics of kindergartens and day-care centers. Indeed, for these scholars' analytical pur-poses to a large extent both types of institutions are similar in major respects: for example, in terms of curriculum and educational goals. But the differences between them bear importance for our analysis. The fact that children attend day-care centers for whole days involves, from an organizational point of view, a much more complex set of tasks which are to be managed and arranged: not only educational activities, but also such things as cooking and eating, preparing for sleep and sleeping, and longer hours over which the children must be monitored. Thus my point is that if, as I have set out to do, one wants to understand the organizational nature of managing the body and emotions, then because of the breadth and complexity of the managerial issues they face, day-care centers are an apt instance through which to do so.

Furthermore, because they cater to children of working mothers, the official view is that these institutions must somehow compen-sate for what the children lack at home. Thus, it is especially in such preschools that assumptions about motherhood, 'natural' child development, and the proper ways of bringing up Japanese children come to the fore. Given the centrality of such notions among middle-class urban Japanese, one would expect that they figure in the way that day-care centers see themselves in relation to parents (primarily mothers) and children. We may better understand, in other words, how these central notions are realized in the concrete organizational arrangements of such establishments. Along these lines, the benefit of studying day-care centers lies in the fact that they allow us to examine the combination of cultural notions of childcare, organized formal care, and body practices.

Why Katsura Day-Care Center?

In this section let me briefly say a few words about the actual case chosen, and why it is suitable for the analysis of the questions I have set out to explore. Between July and September of 1988, and again during September of 1994, I studied the day-care center that forms the primary focus of this study (I also visited about fifteen other preschools). Katsura Day-Care Center is located in the southwestern part of Kyoto (Japan's ancient capital, and a city of one-and-a-half million people). The center's twenty-two teachers (all women) cater for about 110 children between the ages of a few months and six years (although most of the children belong to the older groups of three-, four- and five-year olds). Parents of children are predominantly white-collar company employees, teachers and self-employed people. The school year is divided into three terms of roughly equal length, and runs from April to March.

The suitability of Katsura *Hoikuen* as a case for examining issues related to socialization, organization and embodiment in Japanese preschools, centers on the question of its typicality or the extent to which it is representative of other cases. Unlike Britain or the United States, Japan is marked (as is, for instance, France and Sweden) by rather uniform childcare systems (Robinson *et al.* 1979; Tobin *et al.* 1989: 210, 216; Hendry 1986a: 128; Peak 1989: 95; Kotloff 1988).[2] As a consequence, Katsura *Hoikuen* is very similar to preschools throughout the country in terms of teacher–children ratios and teacher–parent relations, curriculum and activities, tuition levels, administrative control, staffing practices and the kind of ongoing care provided for children. Thus we can safely assume a basic commonality of practices between Katsura *Hoikuen* and other such establishments. Moreover, being an urban center that caters for primarily middle-class parents, Katsura *Hoikuen* is similar in terms of the family background of the children to most centers in Japan. My assumption is thus that the findings of my study are representative of most day-care centers and may be suggestive of Japanese preschools in general.

Yet the detailed analysis of such a case study has other, not inconsiderable, methodological and theoretical advantages beyond its typicality. In the first place, ethnographic case studies allow the careful and sustained exploration of theoretical problems precisely because of the diversity of data on which they are based. Therefore, in order to examine the issues I have set out, I use data gathered from interviews, observations, conversations and educational and administrative texts. On the basis of this diversity of data, I have attempted to examine both formal and informal social processes and to chart and reconstruct organizational practices.

Finally, my analysis should be seen as what Yin (1981: 47–8) terms an exploratory case study – i.e. a single case design that is justified because it serves a revelatory purpose. It serves this purpose in two interrelated senses: by offering insights into a hitherto little explored set of questions and in suggesting further topics for analysis.

On Reading the Book

Let me offer a short synopsis of each chapter in this volume in order to orient prospective readers. The volume consists of eight chapters and five interludes (or addendums) interspersed among them. The aim of these (at times, rather light-hearted) interludes is to illuminate a number of points that are related to socialization in Japanese preschools but are not directly related to the analysis.

Chapter 2 contains a short overview of the day-care system in Japan and a more detailed ethnographic introduction to Katsura *Hoikuen*. The aim of this chapter is to provide a background for the rest of the volume.

In Chapter 3 I deal with the question of how Japanese people add ties and orientations to horizontal groups to the strong dyadic and hierarchical relations nurtured at home. The core of my analysis is devoted to examining the transition of children from the family to preschool. In examining this issue I suggest focusing on naptime as a social form which has its own rules and internal dynamics. Such a conceptualization allows us to examine both the organizational management of sleep, and the ways in which naptime at preschool is related to patterns of putting children to sleep in the home. My contention is that sleeptime at day-care centers is an occasion through which patterns inculcated at home are subtly used – through the management of the body and emotions – in order to convey children from the world of the home to the wider social world.

This chapter is followed by the first interlude that deals (through my own personal experiences) with the different assumptions which underlie sleeping patterns in the Israeli Kibbutz and Japanese day-care centers.

In Chapters 4 and 5 I take both my empirical and theoretical concerns a step further. Theoretically, I explore the manner in which a set of central educational emphases are internalized by the children within preschools. Empirically, I focus on a variety of structured and unstructured educational and play activities. Two of the primary educational goals which Japanese preschools work towards achieving are 'group orientation' or 'group consciousness' (*shudan seikatsu, shudan ishiki*) and 'perseverance' or 'persistence' (*gaman, gambaru*). While the first goal is related to collective activities that take place in preschool, the second is more person or individual centered. In these two chapters I argue that two inter-related theoretical problems are involved in understanding the internalization of these goals. The first is the manner in which preschool practices lead to group life and persistence becoming natural, taken for granted parts of the children's lives. The second problem is the way these emphases gain 'directive', or motivational force. Specifically, the point here is to illuminate the manner in which 'grouping' and 'persevering' become habitual matters *and* acquire motivational significance for the children.

The second interlude comes after Chapter 4. It comprises a short excerpt from Joy Hendry's (1986a) book on preschools, and is devoted to the Japanese version of the three pigs story. Chapter 5 is followed by the third interlude which depicts the 'marathon' held in a Japanese day-care center in the early 1980s and that our son participated in. The aim of these passages is to illustrate educational practices related to group efforts and to persistence.

In Chapter 6, I explore the theoretical issues raised in the previous chapters through a detailed study of mealtimes at the center. My proposal is that while around the world the preparation and consumption of food is used as a major means for the socialization of youngsters, actual mealtime practices vary cross-culturally to fit distinctive notions of proper eating behavior. More specifically, I contend first that in Japanese preschools food is explicitly and implicitly related to inculcating a sense of group belongingness, absorbing notions of responsibility, and learning the organization and aesthetics of 'typical' meals. Second, that imparting eating habits involves harnessing the basic physiological processes of the children so that they gradually master self-control and self-reliance. And third, that teachers mobilize and control mothers in and around food related issues in order to assure the proper implementation of all of these educational goals.

The fourth interlude traces out the background of food practices in institutions of early childhood education in Japan. I focus on how the menus of Japanese preschools are constructed within a wider social context that involves nutritional science, industrial food and notions of natural nourishment.

In Chapter 7 I take the discussion in a new direction altogether to ask some questions about the very bases of our approach to the study of Japanese children. I examine the interrelationships between three elements of Japanese culture: power, play and classification. More specifically, I focus on the behaviors of what Schwartzman (1978: 25) calls the 'child as critic' or what Kishima (1991: 82) would call 'tricksters' in Japanese preschools. It is these children who offer the most concerted resistance to the imposition of teachers' standards of behavior and emotional involvement in the preschool. Most teachers and educators tend to view such critical play behavior in terms of what it is not: not work, not real, not serious, not productive and not contributive. My contention is that much of our social scientific understanding of socialization in general, and in Japan in particular has adopted this view of critical play. In contrast, my argument is that acts of caprice and questioning should be seen as constitutive of preschools to the same degree as their formal organizational hierarchy, division of labor, and curriculum.

The fifth interlude is a short text taken from the work of Catherine Lewis (1989). It illustrates the kind of disciplinary measures commented upon by American observers of Japanese preschools.

In the volume's conclusion, I undertake a more speculative mode of analysis by drawing out some of the wider implications. By situating the book among contemporary studies of Japan I deal with three issues: the organizational context of body projects; the long-term effects of child socialization; and the conceptualization of Japanese selves.

Notes

1 For example, take the notion of emotions: "if there is a mind/body unity and the emotions belong to this unity, they cannot simply be identified with what is irrational as opposed to the rationative properties of the mind. Nor can the body be simply identified with emotion and so itself come to stand for the irrational" (Strathern 1994: 44).

2 In contrast to this view, both Boocock (1989: 42) and DeCoker (1989) mention the diversity of Japanese preschools. While their point is well taken, two matters should be mentioned in this regard: one, Japan, like France, is *relatively* uniform; and two, both Boocock and Decoker explicitly sought the extremes of diversity in their samples. Because of the design of their research they tended to find the outer edges of diversity rather than the vast majority of preschools that are very similar to each other.

Chapter 2

The Institutional Framework
Katsura Day-Care Center

The aim of this chapter is to provide a general overview of the institutional framework within which my case study is placed. I begin with a short description of the social and organizational contexts of day-care centers in Japan, outline the main kind of assumptions which govern the proffering of care in such institutions and introduce the center where I carried out fieldwork. Because other chapters in the volume include substantial ethnographic descriptions of various activities I limit my depiction here to more general points.[1]

Day-Care and Caring Alternatives

The establishment and maintenance of day-care centers in Japan should be understood as the outcome of older government policies of social welfare and the movement of women into the labor market. While Japan has always had a population of working mothers (J. Lebra 1976: 299–300), it was only in the late 1950s that the country – like other industrialized societies (Lupri 1983: 13) – saw a significant growth in the number of women who worked outside the home. The reasons for this trend include the development of a full employment economy in which labor is short; the increased impact of higher education; a decrease in the size of families and improvement of home facilities which have partly freed women from housework; the decline of housework as a meaningful activity; and the need, in many families, for women to supplement household incomes (Yamagata 1986: 3; Pharr 1976:

307; Ikegame 1982: 10). Indeed, women now represent over 40 per cent of the Japanese work force, and almost half of all females beyond the age of fifteen are working either as salaried employees or as family workers (Hayashi 1985). As Carney and O'Kelly (1990: 127–8) note, most of these women make up an important flexible labor reserve that is strategically necessary to the maintenance of the restricted lifetime employment system (which covers only a minority of Japanese workers, primarily men, in the large firms), and to facilitating structural transitions in a rapidly changing economy.

As more and more women have entered the labor force they have encountered difficulties in providing care for their children. These difficulties are related primarily to the changes that have taken place in the extended family. Today, with the nuclearization of the family, fewer households have grandparents who can fulfill the traditional role of caring for preschoolers (Robins-Mowry 1983: 179–81). Moreover, in contrast to the United States where a large part of caretaking is undertaken by babysitters – i.e. home care by a non-relative (Woolsey 1977: 131–2) – such an alternative is still very rare in Japan (Befu 1971: 155; Boocock 1987: 57). Thus Japanese working mothers have increasingly come to depend on institutional support: that is, group care by multiple care-takers.

In the first years after the war most care-taking institutions in the country were operated privately, very often (but not exclusively) in what were called 'baby hotels' (Yamagata 1986: 3). Throughout the 1960s and 1970s considerable attention – on the part of the media, politicians, and welfare officials – was directed at the conditions found in these 'baby hotels' and at their unregulated and profit-seeking activities. It was during these two decades that the number of government-run or government-regulated day-care centers – or day-nurseries as the term *hoikuen* is officially translated – grew considerably. Today, government run centers account for about 60 per cent of the 22,000 centers registered with the Ministry of Health and Welfare (Koseisho 1993). The rest, while privately run, are all officially recognized, regulated and to a large extent sub- sidized. Alongside these institutions are found some special day-care programs attached to large organizations like hospitals or department stores (Creighton 1989: 8). In general, all of these institutions must adhere to nationally set minimum standards cover-ing such matters as equipment, space per child, or teacher–children ratios.

Children and Institutional Care

Boocock (1977: 71) notes that how "a society treats its children depends upon its views of what children are like, as well as upon what is perceived as necessary for the smooth functioning of the society itself". Two basic premises shape the official State view of institutional care-taking in Japan: one about the 'natural' needs of children and the other about the proper loci for their fulfillment. The words of a teacher in the (government run) day-care center our son attended in the early 1980s are typical and instructive in this regard. We talked of the proper age for attending day-care establishments, when she said:

> only from the age of three. Until then it's best for the child to have the affection and love of its mother. This is especially true until the time they've learned to control their bowel movements . . . All in all it's best to be with mother. That's why the children who attend day-care centers are pitiful [*kawaisoo* – also pitiable], they yearn to be with their mothers.

Having observed children at that center and at a number of other establishments, these remarks surprised me. They seemed to contradict other people's (Bettleheim and Takanishi 1976: ch. 10; Roberts 1986: 180–1; Rohlen 1989a: 3; Saso 1990; 121), and my own appraisals of the excellent care the youngsters were receiving, and their general well-being. Yet this view consistently cropped up in all of the interviews I held with staff and municipal welfare officials, as well as in national and local government pronouncements.

When I inquired as to the reasons for this view, I met with the following kind of explanation (see Ben-Ari 1987: 204–5). According to the official view, the child's natural place until the age of three or four is in the home with its mother. Indeed, it is only in close physical contact with the mother and the large amounts of affection that she bestows that the child can develop normally. Espoused by teachers, educational specialists, and governmental officials, this idea is the one which is most widely accepted among the urban middle class of today's Japan (for instance see T.S. Lebra 1976: 139). The view – which is sometimes termed 'neo-traditional' (Pharr 1976) – is, in turn, related to the broader social definitions of the role of married women in Japanese culture. These definitions specify such things as the subordination of women to their husbands or certain behavioral norms they are subject to in public. Their importance lies in the juxtaposition of three principles which bear upon how mothering and child-care are perceived: first, that the woman's natural place is in the home; second, that the mother–wife role is primary and that all other activities be subordinated to it (Pharr 1976: 303); and third, that ideally a child should be in its own home surrounded by her or his family and in close proximity to the mother (Hendry 1984: 106; Fujita 1989: 77). Indeed, so crucial are these conditions for 'natural' development, it is held, that their lack is seen to result in pathologies like juvenile delinquency later on in life[2] (Early Childhood Education Association 1979: 57).

It is on the basis of these maxims that government policies for institutional care-taking rest. According to this perspective, it is only when there is no alternative that the child should be allowed to attend a day-care center. In other words, only when there are no other options the state must take over for the mother and the family. A number of administrative arrangements designed to support day-care centers underscore these assertions. One has to do with the ways in which the clients and activities of day-care centers are classified and categorized bureaucratically. The children who attend day-care facilities are not categorized along with the children who attend the 'normal' half-day kindergartens (*yoochien*) as part of their one or two years of preschooling under the auspices of the Ministry of Education. Rather, they are consistently catalogued – along with orphans and the physically and mentally handicapped – within the framework of the Ministry of Health and Welfare (Ministry of Education, Science and Culture 1981: 2; Ministry of Health and Welfare 1974; Koseisho, 1993).

The specific aims of day-care centers underline further their essential function of serving children in need: day-care centers are welfare institutions (Ministry of Education, Science and Culture 1981: 2), for children "who lack nurture at home," "who lack in familial care," or who "cannot enjoy care at home" (Early childhood Education Association 1979: 11, 19, 75). The assumption here then, is that day-care centers are institutions which cater for neglected or deprived children. Joy Hendry's observations underscore just how strong this perspective is. In Hendry (1984: 7), she cites one of very few places where day-care centers are defined in terms different from the official view: "to meet the needs of the working mothers who are not forced to work for economic reasons but to work for their own choice, as well as those mothers who have to work for economic reasons" (Early Childhood Education Association 1979: 75). Hendry quickly adds, however, that this citation does not imply a universal approval of such sentiments, and that the heads of the day-care centers that she interviewed "expressed the view that their charges would be better off at home".

An official bureaucrat, a representative of the Mothers and Dependents Welfare Division, Children and Families Bureau, of the Ministry of Health and Welfare, notes (Tochio 1986: 2) that new developments in the environment surrounding children – nuclear families, participation by women in the labor market and in societal activities, changes in parents' attitude to child-raising, and an increase in divorces,

> bring about situations in many cases which make it necessary to augment and complement the child-raising function of the family. Against this backdrop, day nurseries are expected to carry out great missions; they are expected to provide appropriate nursing in tune with the developmental stages of children, including their education . . . Further, day nurseries are expected to provide consultation services as measures to aid child-raising in the face of the reduction of child-rearing functions of the family.

To reiterate, day-care centers are not enabling institutions in the sense of enabling women to go out to work to fulfill themselves as a matter of course, but rather compensatory facilities turned to only as a matter of last resort.

Another administrative device that is consonant with the official view is the scale of fees for the centers. In general, fees are set on a scale based on ability to pay. Thus for married women whose husbands provide 'adequate' incomes, the fees are usually the major proportion of any income they can earn (Pharr 1976: 316–7; Saso 1990: 121). The assumptions behind this arrangement are that mother's place is in the home, and that only the economic necessity justifies sending a child to a center. In order to place children in day-care centers, the parents must prove with letters from employers or the tax office that the mother is working or ill. Moreover, government officials that I interviewed said that children of women who work part time are given a lower priority. In fact, in many municipalities (for instance Otsu-shi 1981) one more criterion for admitting children to day-care centers is that there be no healthy grandparents living with them at home.

These circumstances form the background for the perceived

differences between kindergartens and day-care centers. Tobin and his associates (1989: 45) talk about the unspoken yet clear class and status distinctions between these two types of institutions. These are based on the different groups they were historically established to serve: upper- and middle-class children and the children of poor people. But "the class distinction is muddled by growing presence of children of dual-career, high-status professional parents (such as physicians) in *boikuen*" (Tobin *et al.* 1989: 47). My observations are close to Fujita's (1989: 77; see also Roberts 1986: 180) who notes that *boikuen* are less prestigious than *yoochien* and some people express strong reservations about sending children to day-care. Indeed, to this day, the revelation that my boys have gone to day-care centers in Japan, England and Israel tends to be greeted by Japanese people with an uneasy silence or with a sympathetic "well I guess their mother had to work".

Care-Takers: Mother Substitutes to Educators

It is against this background that the caretaker role may be understood. Nursery teachers are seen by themselves and by others not in a custodial role but as comprising two other interrelated roles. Up until about the age of three they are (in a sense) mother substitutes, women acting in place of the children's mothers. Afterwards, there is a subtle shift to a role that is similar to that of kindergarten teachers and they become educators. Thus for the older children, caretakers offer a mixture of mothering and education. Let us take each of these components in turn.

Substitution is predicated on somehow overcoming the artificial separation between mothers and their children. That this is a 'substitutional' rather than a 'custodial' emphasis is illustrated through a stress – *not* taken for granted in other care-taking systems like the American or the Israeli (Rossi 1977: 22–3; Robinson *et al.* 1979: ch. 2; Boocock 1977: 92) – on providing all round care. This means that care in Japanese day-care centers involves a constant accent – like that found in many socialist countries (Robinson *et al.* 1979: ch. 5) – on the moral, educational, and emotional dimensions not only of 'hard' curricula, but also of eating, going to the bathroom, keeping clean, and sleeping (Early Childhood Education Association 1979: 27). These notions are not unlike the ones held by elementary school teachers in Japan who emphasize educating 'whole persons' (Cummings 1980: 12ff). The idea is not one of promoting only cognitive skills in the child's development but of having a strong future orientation with stress on shaping the whole child.

The next excerpt, from an interview with a teacher at a government center, focuses on the special problems of infants:

> In relation to young children who don't yet talk, non-verbal communication is of utmost importance. When they cry, they may be saying that they need to go to the bathroom or something else. Now when this happens when the parents are around they can react, but because the children are at the center for so many hours it's utterly important that *we* be able to react . . . The great problem with the under-threes is that they can't express themselves. Thus there is a need for the teachers to be a substitute for the parents while the children are at the center.

The stress on substitution is perhaps even clearer in the 'mother-like' prescriptions which are given to teachers. The next passage is taken from a semi-official explanation about nursing infants:

> The best thing for the development of emotion at the infant stage is close skin contact with the warm-hearted mother or substitute . . . One teacher should take care of one infant as long as possible, and try to have body contact such as hugging . . . Not only teachers but also parents should show affection directly (Early Childhood Education Association 1979: 57)

But at the age of three a new set of components to the caretaker role emerges. From the time the children are about three, teachers begin to systematically disengage themselves from them and to increasingly take on the role of educators. As we shall see in Chapter 3, the primary aim of this separation is to foster independence in the children and to get them used to group life. Thus from this stage and onwards, much effort is devoted to peer interaction and cooperation within the larger group, without which parents and teachers feel that children would become over-indulged. To develop only within the confines of the nuclear family involves the danger, according to this view, of becoming too selfish, to be overly involved in dyadic ties with the mother (Tobin *et al.* 1989: 201). Thus to develop 'normally' a Japanese child *must* be part of a group. She or he *must* participate in group activities (*shudan seikatsu*). The proper age thought most suitable for this stage is that of three or four. It is for these reasons then, that teachers in day-care centers are generally non-mothering in their relations with children above the age of three.

All of these educational practices are implemented in the context of organizations that are predicated on intervention in children's lives. In order to understand this situation it is essential to take into account first of all, the place of bureaucratic intervention in the lives of 'normal' children: that is, the place of the official design of the lives of youngsters (and their families) who attend the Ministry of Education affiliated or recognized kindergartens from the age of four or five. The official encroachment upon the lives of children is effected through a plethora of mechanisms: for example, talks and lectures to parents, home visits, phone calls or personal meetings with teachers, documentation sent home, (like personal message books or class letters), the use of message boards at preschools, and the participation of parents in PTAs, parents' days and various parties and ceremonies. As Hendry (1984) notes, these efforts are devoted to preparing the future generations of good, cooperative citizens (and, I would add, laborers).

In day-care centers, however, it becomes evident that this massive intervention is taken even further. Three features contribute to this situation: first, direct regulation is extended and carried out in relation to the lives of children who are below the age of four; second, it takes place over longer hours, and in regard to many of the activities not covered by some or all of regular half-day kindergartens (sleeping, eating, toilet training); and third, it is undertaken within the framework of organizations run or inspected by a welfare bureaucracy and not by the local Board of Education. Indeed, Boocock (1989: 46) suggests that though no systematic empirical comparisons have been carried out, there are indications that control at *hoikuen* is greater than at *yoochien*.

Moreover, in Japan certain cultural conceptions tend both to legitimize and to amplify a stress on the official involvement in children's lives. As the 'neo-traditional' or mainstream view would have it, teachers – and still to a great, if contested, measure, bureaucrats – are representatives of the Japanese state. As such representatives they possess certain duties and prerogatives to intervene in and control the private sphere in the name of communal and societal aims. As Dore (1978: 193) eloquently puts it:

No Confucian has recognized the validity of the distinction between public and private morality. No homes are castles in the sense that one can be allowed to do what one likes within them. All moral conduct is of concern to society.

These ideas are actualized in institutions of early childhood education in terms of teachers functioning as overseers of mothers and children for the children's sake. The assumption of the staff at such facilities is that it is their social obligation to intervene in families on behalf of the children and to bestow something on them that will compensate for what is missing at home. A number of observers have noted that day-care teachers continuously try to get mothers to fulfill their role. For instance, teachers discourage mothers from shopping after work before picking up their children: it is thought the sooner the pick-up the better for the parent–child relationship, (Sano 1989: 128; Ben-Ari 1987). Fujita (1989: 78) talks of a head teacher who complained that:

> There is no point in telling them [mothers], because they are not going to change. Some mothers pick up their children after doing their grocery shopping for supper. Being mothers, I would think they would naturally want to see their children as soon as possible after work. Therefore, they should come and pick them up before going shopping. Besides, taking children shopping is itself educational.

Let me now turn to the specific center that I studied.

The Katsura Day-Care Center

Katsura *Hoikuen* (Day-Care Center) is a private Christian affiliated institution located in the southwestern side of Kyoto not far from the Emperor's summer palace. In caters for 110 children between the ages of three months and six years, with a staff of 22 full-time teachers and one part-time employee in the kitchen. Most of the youngsters belong to the groups of three-, four-, and five-year old children. While I indicate ways in which Katsura *Hoikuen* differs from other centers in Japan, the following point should be taken into account. In contrast to other societies – like China or the United States – and like others – such as France or Sweden – Japan is marked by a relative uniformity in the child-care system throughout the country (see Robinson *et al.* 1979; Tobin *et al.* 1989: 210, 216; Hendry 1986a: 128; Peak 1989: 95; Kotloff 1988). As a consequence, Katsura *Hoikuen* is very similar to preschools throughout the country in terms of teacher–children ratios and teacher–parent relations, curriculum and activities, tuition levels and administrative control, and the kind of ongoing care provided for children.

Katsura Day-Care Center is considered a medium-sized institution among establishments whose size range between 60 and 180 children. Municipalities differ in the proportion of government run day-care centers they contain, and Katsura is one of the 226 privately run *hoikuen* in Kyoto. It is not one of the 35 government day-care centers that provide service to handicapped youngsters, to children of Burakumin or Korean parents or to welfare cases. Indeed, according to municipal ward officials (Kyoto is divided into administrative wards), Katsura *Hoikuen* is very typical of urban institutions in the city both in terms of average parents' incomes and their occupations. Parents of children are predominantly white-collar company employees, teachers and self-employed people.

During the time of this study, the head of the center and her deputy were in the midst of attempting to introduce activities related to the Montessori method. While this move has weakened in the ensuing years (the deputy head related this to me by phone), the reasons for the initial efforts are indicative of wider developments in Japan. The demographic trends of shrinking numbers of children have led to a situation in which there is heightened competition between preschools. While this competition was at first limited to kindergartens, the increasing number of working mothers has led to a situation in which many day-care centers also compete for a dwindling number of children. Much of this competition – part of what Tobin and his associates (1989: 175ff.) term the 'business of preschool'– is centered on attracting children to institutions on the basis of their distinctive characteristics (under what in the world of marketing would be called a process of 'product differentiation'). During fieldwork I visited or heard of kindergartens and day-care centers offering such distinctive additions as English conversation, music education, sports and swimming, drawing and painting, 'free play', or mixed age groups education (*tatte-wari kyooiku*) (see also Hendry 1986a: 63, 126; Kotloff 1988; DeCoker 1989: 56–7). The stress on the Montessori method at Katsura *Hoikuen* should be seen in this light; it is not a true Montessori preschool as hardly any of the teachers have been trained according to these methods and only some of the equipment is found there. Katsura *Hoikuen* is thus actually very similar – in terms of educational practices and goals – to preschools around the country.

Japan has over 1500 Christian affiliated institutions of early childhood education. Many parents find these institutions attractive because they have a good reputation for reliable and conscientious education and care (Ishigaki 1987: 161). The overwhelming majority of parents, however, are not themselves and do not want their children to become Christians (cf. Hendry 1986a: 63). Moreover, religiously affiliated preschools in Japan are quite common – in Kyoto, according to informants, they are especially widespread – with the majority of such establishments belonging to Buddhist temples.

All of the full-time staff (including the two cooks) are women who are licensed day-care center teachers with at least two years of education beyond the high school level. In addition, all have passed a qualifying examination set by local government. The center's deputy head has an MA in education from a Kyoto university. Most of the teachers are in their twenties, two are in their thirties, two in their forties, and the head is in her early sixties. Each year as many as six out of the twenty-two teachers leave to marry or to have children. The center also employs (as a welfare measure) a young man who suffers from autism. The young age of the majority of teachers serves to keep Japanese preschools afford-able (Tobin *et al.* 1989: 216–7): as salaries in day-care centers (like salaries in most Japanese organizations) are linked to years of service, the short careers of most preschool teachers (3–6 years) keep down personnel costs which are the biggest outlay in most preschool budgets. As the head of the center admitted during an interview, it makes sense to employ young women with relatively little experience as they are paid less. Staffing patterns thus also reflect conceptions of gender. This is a relatively low paid job which is often seen – by men *and* women – as suitable to the 'natural' inclinations of women. Where one does find men in the preschool systems, they are usually heads of institutions or bureaucrats assigned to government sections dealing with child-care.

Katsura *Hoikuen* is also a teaching institution. Although run as an autonomous establishment, it maintains organizational links with a nearby teachers' training school. Once a week students from this school come to one of the classes at the center to direct an activity and to help with the cleaning and administrative chores of the staff. From the children's point of view this situation implies that the presence of students is very much part of the everyday life of Katsura *Hoikuen*. Organizationally this means that like a teaching hospital, so here the head, her assistant, and (to a lesser extent) the class teachers are constantly occupied with supervising and appraising students.

The *hoikuen* is a two-story structure built in the mid-1980s and includes an entrance hall where one sheds outside shoes for indoor shoes or slippers. The large doors are open all day as though to underscore the easy movement of children in and out of the center. The only places which are off-limits to the children are the kitchen, storerooms and the small teachers' meeting and changing room. The children often wander into the office (equipped with the latest photocopy and fax machines, and computer) to say hello and then wander off. The top floor houses the rooms of the infants, while the bottom floor contains the rooms of older groups (above the age of three) and the hall which is used for a variety of assemblies, parties and activities. Being an urban center it suffers from a problem common to most urban *hoikuen*: a relative lack of space. Bunched up in the small yard are a tiny garden, slides, jungle-jim, and narrow storage spaces. Trips and hikes are taken to the grounds of a nearby kindergarten located in a Buddhist temple (which has large grounds), to the picnic areas in Arashiyama, along the streets of the neighborhood (to see trains and traffic signals, or the leaves that have fallen in fall), and to the fire-fighting station in the area.

Katsura *Hoikuen* prescribes no uniforms either for the children or for the caretakers (unlike some other day-care centers and many kindergartens). The head of the center told me that this was done to give the children a feeling that it is easy to play at the center, and to give them opportunities to choose the colors they like. Yet for all of this everyone tends to dress in similar manner: for example in summer, teachers in track-pants and T-shirts, and the children in shorts and T-shirts.

The six age groups are named after flowers (for example tulip, violet or dandelion). The ratio of children per teacher runs from three infants for every caretaker in the group of one year-old babies through to twenty-five children and the class teacher in the group of six year-old children. As in other centers (Fujita 1989: 81) there is very little flexibility in attendance, and the children are expected to attend every school day and for at least seven or eight hours. In keeping with municipal policy almost every class has a number of handicapped children who are integrated as much as possible into the activities of the center.

A Typical Day

'Typicality' and 'representation' are contested terms in contemporary social science. Their contested nature lies in approaches that stress individual occurrences, the specialness of situations. Yet for all of this stress, social life is made up of recurring rhythms and patterns. Hence in this section let me briefly describe a typical day at Katsura *Hoikuen*. Such days are typical in the sense of the sheer statistical frequency of their occurrence. But they are also typical in terms of being the standard against which the specialness of other days – the monthly birthday parties or yearly sports day – are measured and constructed. The typical day is very similar to those days richly documented by Peak (1991a) and Hendry (1986a) and to the days I witnessed during visits to about fifteen centers in the Kyoto and Osaka areas.

Although the *hoikuen* formally opens at seven thirty, the first teachers begin to arrive just after seven. The children – mostly sons and daughters of women who work a distance from the area – begin to trickle in at around twenty past seven. The hours at which children are brought from and then returned home are dependent on rhythms of mothers' workplaces. The youngsters are brought by mothers, fathers, or grandparents by foot, on bicycles or in cars. Each child brings a small bag containing her or his chopsticks, a change of clothing and underwear, and a small notebook for communication between teachers and parents. They stop to shed their shoes at the entrance and then proceed to their respective classrooms to hang up their bags and place the clothing in personal drawers. Sometimes parents – mostly mothers – exchange a few words with the teachers.

The children are free to take out toys, to play outside or to take part in activities and games prepared by teachers (for instance, jigsaw puzzles, painting or card games). Teachers change the kinds of toys and equipment they provide the children according to the latter's perceived abilities. The children often enter the class rooms of other age groups and it is quite common to see children of different ages playing together. These kinds of activities usually go on until nine o'clock when most of the pupils have arrived and settled in. During this time, the teachers also arrive (their attendance is staggered so that between nine and five the majority of teachers are present), stamp their attendance in a special notebook, change clothes and join the children. Some of them use this time for last minute preparations for the day's main program. The two cooks begin their work at eight.

The day's designated monitors – *otooban* – stamp attendance in each child's notebook (in some classes the children do this for themselves). They also ring bells or call their friends to cluster for morning assembly, the formal beginning of the day. Before assembly – actually an activity comprised of a gathering within each class and a congregation of the older three groups – all of the children and the teachers tidy and clean up. Equipment is returned to its place, garbage is collected, chairs and tables prepared for the next activity, and the members of the class are slowly gathered.

During class gatherings the children sit facing the teacher. In many cases there is a set seating order that the children are asked to keep to. In this way if a child is especially noisy or troublesome teachers simply change their seating position as a means to quieten them down. The teacher reads out the register of names, and the class members answer in a loud and clear voice, and if they do not perform this in a proper way they are asked to do so again. It is in these opportunities that children are expected to learn to control their voices and behavior (Peak 1989: 105). Teachers then ask the *otooban* to count the number of children present and absent and to report the number of children and teachers who need to be served lunch. Next, a round of ritual greetings – collective declarations of 'Good Morning' addressed to other groups and to teachers and accompanied by bows – are led by the daily monitors. This activity is followed by receiving guests (students from the seminary or the anthropologist, for example) and a few songs until the assembly of the three groups of older children or the morning activity is ready. Very often teachers take this opportunity to talk about what is going to take place that day.

The larger morning assembly takes place about three or four times a week and is invariably led by the center's deputy head. The sixty or seventy children of the older three groups gather in the hall bringing their chairs with them. Although the children sit in their respective class groupings there is no set pattern of sitting within groups. Here class monitors report the number of children present, ritual greetings are recited (sometimes by all of the children and sometimes in groups), guests are welcomed and a morning prayer is said. In addition, songs are sung (often to the accompaniment of an organ or piano) and almost always a story told. The stories are of a general nature or based on various biblical themes as adapted to the local context (the plots invariably revolve around issues of giving thanks, cooperation or kindness). Morning assemblies rarely last more than thirty or forty minutes.

The main morning programs (described and analyzed in Chapter 4) include arts and crafts projects, rhythmics classes, swimming, Montessori exercises, musical undertakings, or (more rarely) card and box games. Participation in these programs, which are carried out almost all of the time in the framework of class groupings, is for all intents and purposes compulsory and teachers make active efforts to involve all of the children. There is almost no direct academic orientation at base of these programs. As in other Japanese preschools (Peak 1991a: 194), so at Katsura *Hoikuen*, and in *all* of the centers that I visited, reading and writing were not taught to the children. To be sure, reading and writing are the result of the children's natural curiosity and teachers often react to their pleas to show them how to write a specific character, or to read out a specific word, but these practices are not part of the formal curriculum.

Space in classrooms – as in other preschools (Sano 1989: 129) – is multi-purpose. Classrooms are usually empty until the teachers and children take out the toys or equipment, or arrange the chairs and tables for a specific activity. Thus the impression is of a constant circulation of people, chairs and tables, toys and play-things, equipment and materials throughout the day. This kind of arrangement stands in contrast to many American and British centers where certain areas or corners of rooms are set up per-manently for particular uses. The situation in Japan also implies that almost every movement from one activity to another involves coordinating the activities of all of the children of a specific group.

The next important activities are lunch and naptime (examined in Chapters 6 and 3). After sleeping the children eat a light snack and then prepare to return home. They prepare their bags and gather in class groups for the final assembly. During these gatherings teachers name the following day's monitors, songs, and remind the children of any special activities that will take place in the near future. These are also occasions for reflecting about the activities in the class during the day. Teachers often use these opportunities to talk about such things as quarrels between children, the importance of making up and the enjoyment of participating in various activities.

Afternoons are devoted to free play in a manner that is very similar to what goes on before morning assembly. This period takes place between half-past three and six o'clock (the formal closing time of the center). When children are fetched they take their bags, and go through a ritual of separation from teachers and other children. These periods, more than in the mornings, are opportunities for parents and teachers to exchange a few words about problems related to children, or to more general goings on at the center. Towards five thirty the remaining teachers (those who had arrived early that day have already left) and children begin to clear and clean up.

It is against the background of cycles of typical days that special events that punctuate the yearly calendar take place. These events include monthly birthday parties and outings, and yearly occurrences like the sports field day, Christmas party, rice-cake making meeting, art exhibition, Respect for the Aged Day ceremonies, parents' participation day, bazaar and entry and graduation ceremonies. In addition, there are special programs integrated into regular days devoted to such topics as the changing of the seasons, modern and ancient festivals or historical incidents (the bombing of Hiroshima). On these days special talks are often given to the children and songs taught and learnt. Other times teachers take opportunities like the visit of an anthropologist from Israel to talk about the Middle East (a large map was shown), the length of time it takes to fly to Japan from different places in the world and the character of universities ('big schools').

This chapter provides the essential background for an understanding of Katsura *Hoikuen*. In the following chapters I explore in depth the theoretical issues raised in the introduction.

Notes

1 An extended description of the day-care center and its wider social and governmental circumstances can be found in Ben-Ari (forhcoming).
2 The continued acceptance of this view is attested to in a survey carried out by the Ministry of Health and Welfare in 1991:

> Among the female respondents, 52% thought that women should leave their jobs after giving birth and resume work when the children were older, an increase of 10 percentage points over the 1982 survey. Only 18% felt that women should continue working even after they gave birth, a slight rise of 3 points . . . The results indicate that many women continue to hold a traditional image of the family, one that centers on children (Japan Topics, 1992).

Chapter 3

From Mothering to Othering
Organization, Culture and Naptime

Introduction

Every society faces the problem of transferring the set of identities, commitments and sentiments that center on the family to a set focused on some wider group or groups. In all of the industrial societies this transfer involves the movement of children into the system of formal education, usually preschools. Comparatively speaking however, Japan presents something that is especially problematic in this regard. Shields (1989) suggests that because of the intense indulgence of Japanese mothers, many observers are mystified by the relative ease of the transition of pupils from the highly charged home context to the fully demanding classroom environment. Lewis (1989: 140; see also Peak 1991a: 186) asks about the ways in which 'indulged' undisciplined toddlers become attentive and well-disciplined schoolchildren in large classes where subordination of personal needs to group goals is often the dominant norm. Tobin, Wu and Davidson (1989: 204) elaborate further by noting that at

> home Japanese children learn to love and be loved, they learn the ways of dependence (*amae*), they learn dyadic interpersonal skills, and they learn to have an ease in spontaneous interactions in the bosom of their families. But to learn to enjoy ties to peers, to learn to transfer some of the warmth of parent–child relations to other relationships, to learn to balance the spontaneity enjoyed at home (*honne*) with formality (*tatemae*), emotion with control, and family with society, to learn to become, in

other words, truly Japanese, the child must be given a chance to move beyond the walls of the home to more complex social interactions. In today's Japan, for most children, these more complex interactions are found first in preschools.

The problem thus appears to be one of contradictory forces working within the home and within the preschool. On the one hand, research on child rearing practices has consistently found what are by any Western standards very strong relations of dependency between caretakers (that is, mothers) and children (Doi 1973; Kumagai 1981; Conroy *et al.* 1980; Hess *et al.* 1980). These hierarchical and dyadic relations are intentionally promoted by mothers who actively seek to create ties of dependency with their children through such practices as co-bathing, co-sleeping, non-verbal communications, or indulging their desires (see Lebra 1976; Tanaka 1984). On the other hand a very wide range of psychological, sociological, and anthropological studies have shown the (again, comparatively speaking) strong group orientation of Japanese people (Befu 1971; Rohlen 1989a; Fuller *et al.* 1986). This orientation finds its expression in such matters as strong horizontal ties, commitment to and investment in group activities, identification with collective bodies and a basic embeddedness and 'comfortableness' in groups (Tobin *et al.* 1991; Hendry 1986b). This kind of orientation is said to be expressed in such entities as school classes or work groups.

Along these lines we may ask the question which will guide the analysis in this chapter: how do the Japanese – and by this I mean members of the urban middle-class – utilize, transfer, or add to the strong dyadic and hierarchical ties nurtured at home, the wider horizontal ties and orientations to a group? To put this by way of a play on words, how is the 'm' in mothering put in parenthesis so that children add othering to (m)othering.

In this chapter, I argue that many studies of early childhood education in Japan suggest a complex model of children's growing abilities to handle – to distinguish between, and to undertake the behavior appropriate to – the two categories of 'home' and 'preschool'. While these studies well illuminate how cultural ideals are actualized in families and in institutions of early childhood education, they do not specify how and why the classification between home and preschool is adopted by the children and then used in subsequent situations. In other words, because they seem to assume that cultural definitions and classifications are somehow automatically learnt, the link between culture and motivation is left unexamined. I contend that a focus on what Abu-Lughod and Lutz (1990: 12) term 'embodied experiences' – experiences that involve the whole person, including the body – helps us understand the process by which cultural distinctions are internalized. In this manner we may understand how what is learnt at home and at preschool becomes compelling to the children, or – to borrow from Strauss (1992: 1) – how these cultural messages 'get under the children's skins'.

I propose to examine these issues through a focus on 'naptime' at Katsura *Hoikuen*. In order to justify my focus on this phenomenon, I need to answer three questions: Why day-care centers; why sleep; why sleep in day-care centers?

Naptime and Preschools

As I showed in the previous chapter, for a variety of reasons – primarily related to the entry of women into the labor force (Hayashi 1985; Yamagata 1986; Carney and O'Kelly 1990) – a substantial part of primary socialization in Japan takes place within preschools. In Japan, institutions of early childhood education are differentiated into *yoochien* (kindergartens) and *hoikuen* (day-care centers). Kindergartens are usually open half-days and cater for children aged four and five. Day-care centers normally operate for a whole day (often from seven in the morning until six at night). They cater to children of working mothers between the ages of a few months and six (in reality most of the children attend only after the age of two). In the past two decades, day-care centers have shown the greatest rate of growth. Today there are 22,000 public or publicly recognized day-care centers that cater for over 2 million children (Koseisho 1993). Consequently, these organizations are becoming increasingly important in preparing children simultaneously for the educational system and for the workforce.

Why sleep? In a ground-breaking work based on research carried out in the 1960s, Caudill and Plath (1986: 247) point out that if "a third of our life is passed in bed, with whom this time is spent is not a trivial matter". As they propose, co-sleeping customs seem to be consonant with major interpersonal and emotional patterns of family life in a culture. But because of its special character, sleep is more than an important manifestation of emotions and social relations. Sleep is marked by fragility and fracturability. Sleep is probably *the* phenomenon of release from pressures. People are released not only from external pressures like social ties and demands (roles), but also from the internal pressures of our psychological forces. Sleep, in other words, allows us to retreat from everything that is 'objectively' and 'subjectively' social (Schwartz 1973: 20). Take the plethora of rules that surround the sleeping person: for example, where and when to sleep, or with whom and how one can be disturbed. In terms of the release of internal forces, sleep and the period just before sleep are relatively open to the rise of associations, thoughts, and memories whether they be pleasurable or unpleasant (Pope 1978; Csikszentmihalyi and Graef 1975).

Along these lines, we may begin to understand why it may be interesting to examine the place of sleep in day-care centers. On a technical level we know that preparations for and the sleep period itself take about two out of the eight or ten hours that the children spend at the center. This means that between 20–25% of the children's time at the day-care center is devoted to sleeping activities. Moreover, naptime is something that occurs on the majority of days the children attend preschool. The justification for dealing with the theme of sleep is not just quantitative. It is related to the quality – the special fragility and fracturability – of this activity.

A review of the general literature about institutions of early childhood education reveals that sleeptime is one of the most common periods during which problems arise (see Provence *et al.* 1977: 130–3). For example, from the point of view of the educational institution, problems of adjustment are often expressed in terms of too little or too much sleep. During naptime many of the children's tensions and apprehensions – whether they be related to the home or to the center – may emerge. For instance, some children may re-experience the separation from parents during this time, while others may remember fights or scuffles they have had during the day.

Here then is my thesis: an examination of the organizational treatment of sleep (and sleep related activities) may illuminate some of the problems of 'managing' the movement of children between home and the wider world. It may be illuminating because it is in and around this issue where one finds strong family patterns, that preschools find it most difficult to manage the movement out of the home. Thus an examination of naptime as an intersection of institutional arrangements and embodied experience may clarify how the children's emerging sense of distinctions between the family and the outside world is internalized.

Sleeptime at Katsura Day-Care Center

Preparations for sleep at Katsura Day-Care Center begin around noon in the hall where the children of the older groups sleep. The children and the teachers clean the hall in which morning activities took place (for instance, morning assembly, games, or arts and crafts). Next, long mats (actually underbedding) are rolled out onto the floor, and then starting from the walls and working their way inside, teachers and children spread *futon* (thick quilts that serve as mattresses) and blankets around the hall. These beddings are kept in cupboards along the side of the hall (like in homes) during the day and taken home once a week to be cleaned by the children's parents. While each child has her or his *futon*, there is no set place where it is put every day. Rather, the place where the three groups sleep and the location of each child within the group change everyday. Each child is encouraged, based on their individual ability, to help with the preparations.[1] At times, with no prompting from the caretakers, a few of the older girls assist younger children during these preparations. The teachers close the curtains and turn on the airconditioners in summer or the heaters in winter, and the children are invited to go to their home rooms for lunch.

Upon finishing lunch around 12:30 the children begin preparing for sleep. Under the supervision of the teachers, they go to the toilet, wash their hands and brush their teeth (in the summer shower), and put on their pyjamas. Subsequently, the children enter the hall to wait, somersault or play tag until everyone has arrived. They then sit down to listen to stories told by teachers. Following this activity, teachers often play the piano or some quiet music on a cassette recorder (rarely will they sing songs that activate the children). While all of this is going on, the lights are gradually turned off, and a number of times I saw the same girls from the group of six year-olds beginning to put children from the younger groups to sleep. Then about four or five teachers start to put the children to sleep.

Each child is attended to by being told 'good night' (*oyasumi nasai*) and being tucked in. Teachers are careful to wrap the blankets around the children with only their heads protruding. The teachers move around the children, sit in between two or three and very gently stroke them. At times teachers softly pat the children on their backs or stomachs in a series of onomatopoeically termed *ton-ton-ton* taps, which very often induce them to sleep. If some children create a disturbance they are signalled to stop or very softly whispered at to be quiet. At this stage a number of the children are already asleep, while others sing or talk to themselves or play with their fingers.

A few minutes before one o'clock, the teachers begin to circulate and devote their attention to children who are having trouble falling asleep. Usually they lie next to these children and softly stroke or caress them. Those troublesome ones who are *kappatsu* (sprightly) find that the teachers very delicately but firmly place their heads below their breasts and their behinds under the adults' knees to calm them. At this stage many teachers actually lie next to the children underneath the latters' blankets with full body contact and the exchange of body heat between adults and youngsters. By twenty past one, almost all of the children are asleep and some of the teachers catch a quick nap as well.

While the children are asleep, the teachers undertake a variety of organizational activities such as preparing the equipment needed for the next day's activities; writing diaries and letters sent to parents; filling out forms and documents required by the day-care center; rehearsing for performances at birthdays; holding a variety of meetings either with parents or, much more commonly, with other teachers.

At about two thirty the teachers begin waking the children by gradually turning on the lights. Here again, soft background music often accompanies the teachers who delicately stroke the children, say 'good morning' (*ohayo gozaimasu*), and talk with them about their nap. Some of the teachers lie down next to children who have difficulty awaking and ease their way back into wakefulness. The whole atmosphere is marked by a cozy warmth and tenderness. The teachers often tell the early risers to have patience (*gamman*) for their friends who are having trouble waking up. After the children have risen, the pre-sleep ritual is carried out in reverse: a visit to the toilet; change of clothing; arranging the *futon* (again to the children's ability and with the older girls sometimes helping younger children); a light snack; brushing the teeth and afternoon activities.

Sleep and Home

What happens during the period I have been describing? What is rather obvious is that there are a number of processes that structure the movement between the states of 'wakefulness' and 'sleep' (and later back to 'wakefulness'). These processes involve the arrangements of the hall and the preparation of groups and individual children. In essence, they gradually convey or conduct each child to sleep by reducing external stimuli, and perform a 'ritual'-like sequence of structured and familiar activities (see Winnicott 1971: 2).[2]

Yet there is still something about the activities I have described that, when put in a comparative perspective, seems unique to Japan. I refer to the physically intimate nature of the caresses, the body-to-body contact, and the transfer of body heat between adults and children, all of which take place within formal organizations. This manner of putting to sleep is perhaps what in a variety of cultural contexts would be termed 'mother-like'. Indeed, when I asked the teachers about this matter they often admitted that these patterns were borrowed from home and from the family. One teacher explained that the method of putting the children to sleep at the center,

> may have developed in the past. It's called *soine*, which means to lie [down] with the child like the Chinese ideograph for river. The ideograph is made up of three lines and it's like the child sleeping in between two parents. In *soine* you also have the *futon* which allows you to comfort the children if they cry at night.

These kinds of responses led me to wonder whether it would not be worthwhile to explore what happens at home in order to understand what happens at the center. In this way we can examine how (if at all) some kind of continuity between home and day nursery is constructed and maintained, and how this continuity is (in turn) related to wider assumptions about childcare in Japan.

Starting with Caudill and Plath's (1986) pioneering work, a host of commentators have noted the Japanese preference for co-sleeping in families: in general, children tend to sleep in the same room as their parents. According to this pattern, a child sleeps with its mother until the next child is born, and then she or he relocates to sleep with the father or one of the grandparents (Vogel 1963:

231; Smith and Wiswell 1982: 213). It is not unusual for this pattern to continue until the child reaches the age of ten (Caudill and Plath 1986: 257; Befu 1971: 154–5). To be clear, such 'overcrowding' is not a function of lack of space, because even when there are enough rooms for all of the family's members, many families prefer to sleep in the same room (Caudill and Plath 1986: 247). Indeed, research that has been carried out since the 1960s attests to the continuity of this pattern (see Mizushima, 1975; Morioka 1973; Ishigaki 1987: 166; Lebra 1984: 176; Hendry 1986a: 44; and Coleman 1983: 177).[3]

The routines of many Japanese homes promote this pattern both in terms of the 'proper' place for sleeping and the type of bedding used. Japanese couples frequently sleep with their children between them,

> because it is considered 'natural' and 'good' to do so. From a very early age an American child is expected to become aware of the special relationship between his parents by the existence of the master bedroom with its double bed, by watching their intimate interaction, and by knowing that after a certain hour in the evening he is sent to his own room so that the adults can spend time together. Japanese children experience nothing of the sort, and the mother and her young child are often thought inseparable twenty-four hours a day (Tanaka 1984: 231).

Moreover, not only do children and parents often sleep in the same room, they often sleep on *futon*. These mattresses are stored during the day, and spread out in the middle of the room with their edges almost touching during the night. In this way a parent can rather easily reach out to calm or comfort a child, and a youngster, in turn, can readily roll over and join the parent on her *futon* (see Lebra 1976: 141).

The contrast between *futon* and bed as suitable places for sleep is instructive. A bed, following Caudill and Plath (1986: 267), is a separate container, an immobile receptacle. Beds usually have clear boundaries which differentiate between fixed identities. In addition, beds are usually placed at a distance from each other and for children are situated in a room separated from adults. Finally, beds are usually heavy and not amenable to easy movement. In these circumstances, caretaking often involves an effort on the part of parents who must get up and out of bed (usually moving to another room) in order to attend to their children.

These differences are related, in turn, to what cultures define as proper developmental goals for children. In most of the urban middle-class cultures of the West the notion of sleeping in one's 'proper' place is related to the inculcation of independence in children. Babies are often moved quite early to their own room (maybe even at the earliest possible occasion) in order that they will become independent, and so that the parents may be able to enjoy some 'free' time of their own (Hendry 1986a: 21). In Japan the emphasis is, by contrast, on the promotion of increasing dependence of the child on others, and primarily on the mother. In short, the stress in Japan is on cultivating mutual dependence not independence (see also Tanaka 1984: 232–3). "In Japan, the path seems to lead toward increasing interdependence with other persons, whereas in America the path seems to lead toward increasing independence from others" (Caudill and Plath 1986: 269). Along these lines, sleeping in proximity to parents or on the same *futon* allows the creation of what the Japanese positively value as a sense of secure intimacy. According to this view, co-sleeping contributes to the fostering of dependence by reducing children's anxieties and anticipating their needs and desires.[4]

Furthermore, according to the logic of this view, promotion of dependency within the family is not predicated only on the proximity of parent and child. What is needed is actual physical contact "which is seen as a natural expression of affection, which is desirable and necessary for the proper rearing of children" (Vogel 1963: 232). This contact is seen as essential for the natural development of children. A word borrowed from English is used to characterize this essential physical contact: *sukinshippu* (skinship) (Lebra 1976: 138; 1984: 174–80; Hendry 1986a). Skinship is involved in a variety of activities including not only co-sleeping but also breast-feeding, co-bathing and patterns of nonverbal communication.

Day-Care Centers And Sleep

What then happens in the day-care center? One (initial) interpretation would be that during sleeptime, the teachers function as sort of mother substitutes. According to this interpretation, in enacting their relation the teachers and the children use certain patterns that belong to the domain of the family. Indeed, when I confronted teachers with this interpretation they granted that they may, from one perspective, be seen as mother substitutes (*okaasan-gawari*). But things are actually more complex because teachers are not mother substitutes and perhaps more importantly do not see themselves as mother substitutes for children above the age of three. This notion should be understood as part of the prevalent ideas about the role of day-care centers as institutions of early childhood education.

Whenever I asked day-care teachers about this role, I received a rather standard answer: the primary role of such institutions, I was told, is to teach children 'how to live' (*seikatsu dekiru*), how to become social beings in Japanese society. When pressed to be more specific, teachers talked about day-care centers as developing certain skills and characteristics that are related both to the independent functioning of children (dressing, eating, or talking, for example), and as developing certain sentiments of belonging and social relations (I will go into these points in greater detail in the following two chapters).

In putting these goals into effect, institutions of early childhood education (and by extension schools) are seen as organizations that stand in contrast to the family. They grant children something that is missing at home. To put this rather crudely, most parents, educators and government representatives in contemporary Japan believe that to cultivate a 'true' Japanese character is only possible, if in addition to the family, children undergo experiences within the framework of formal institutions of education: preschools and schools (Tobin *et al*. 1989: 58). To develop only within the confines of the nuclear family involves the danger of becoming too selfish, to be overly involved in dyadic ties with the mother. In order to develop the proper awareness of 'who am I?' – what may be termed a 'sense of self' – a Japanese child *must* be part of a group: she or he *must* participate in group activities (*shudan seikatsu*). The proper age thought most suitable for joining these activities is three or four. It is for these reasons that teachers in kindergartens and day-care centers are rigorously nonmothering in their relations with children, and especially with children above the age of three (Tobin *et al*. 1989: 62).

More generally, this view is related to the attempt at granting children institutional versions of the 'traditional' extended family, or the village or neighborhood communities of yesteryear. The belief is that in the past it was in these contexts that the Japanese developed their group orientation. Japanese preschools thus "function not to destabilize or transform traditional Japanese child rearing but to compensate for features of traditional family and social life lost in the unsettling changes of the postwar era" (Tobin *et al.* 1989: 222). In this sense, teachers are representatives of society who operate preschools as compensatory mechanisms.[5]

Why is it then that during naptime the behavior of teachers resembles that of mothers? My contention is that patterns of putting children to sleep should not be seen at one point of time, but along a longer time scale: along a whole year or along the three years before the children go to school. If we look at the patterns in this way, we will see that the teachers gradually *wean* the children from practices cultivated at home. Let me give four indicators of this process of weaning. One, a long-term view reveals that teachers tend to be more 'mothering' to the younger than to the older children: for instance, according to my field notes the children of the group of three year-old children received many more caresses than did the children of the older two groups. Two, teachers tended to 'co-sleep' (that is, lie down and maintain body contact) with these youngsters more than with the older ones. Three, even among the group of younger children (the three year-olds), 'motherly' patterns decrease as the year progresses (here my data is based on teachers' accounts in interviews). Finally four, by the time the children are ready to go to school they are completely weaned from taking naps at the center.[6]

Sleep, Emotions and the Peer Group

But weaning the children from familial patterns is only part of the story. While I have been discussing dyadic ties – the mother–child and teacher–child bonds – up to this point, it is time to turn to the place of the peer group during naptime. In this respect, teachers appear to recognize the power of ties binding children and mothers, but do not see these ties (as perhaps, would some Western observers) as negative. Rather, they seek ways of directing these bonds towards a wider group. The governing assumption of the teachers is that it is prudent to create an environment within which the strong ties of dependency developed at home are used as a base for creating ties of dependency with the child's peer group.

I suggest that these effects should be understood in terms of the relationship between naptime practices and the children's inner experiences. Since discussion of inner experiences may appear to some readers to be a rather 'murky' subject, let me begin with a set of observable details. One, each child sleeps on a *futon* without any clear boundaries, and with the ready possibility of verbal and physical contact with other children. In fact, the children often do reach out to touch, and occasionally may exchange a few quiet words with their neighbors. Two, the teachers are careful not to devote too much attention to any one child and constantly move between members of each group. Indeed, during interviews, two teachers explicitly mentioned their wariness of showing any kind of favoritism when putting the children to sleep. Three, while the children do not have a set place within their group and the group itself does not have a fixed place in the hall the children are *always* steered towards sleeping with their peers.[7]

Within these circumstances, I would argue, during the twilight period just before falling asleep the children undergo an experience of sinking, of being submerged in their peer group. During these moments, all of their senses – touch, hearing, vision, smell – are transmitting messages to them of immersion in a 'sea' of other children, those very children with whom they interact and play throughout the day. Some of the following are examples of the, again, observable indicators I have recorded for this 'sinking': changes in voice register and language – the children speak quietly and often intimately with their peers; posture and body comportment – they often look into the eyes or enter the personal space of their peers; smell – through the ability to sense their friends' breaths and body odors; and touch – they often come in contact with their playmates or hold their hands. Moreover, it is within the general ambience of naptime that they exhibit – *without* fear of sanction or control – many private behaviors performed before sleep such as finger sucking, singing, playing with their fingers, or touching different parts of their bodies. This is no mean point, because despite the fragility and fracturability of sleep, for the majority of children, the atmosphere during naptime is relaxed enough for resting with their peers.

To be sure, many of these kinds of behaviors can be found in preschools the world over. Thus an American reader of an earlier version of this chapter rightly pointed out that thumb-sucking, smelling other children, and feeling comfortable enough to sleep as at home can also be found in American day-care centers. What I would emphasize is that the distinctive quality of the Japanese case seems to center on the combination of the close physical intimacy between the children, and the fact that the patterns found at the center are consistent with familial patterns.

The significance of these circumstances lies in the relation of naptime to the construction of emotions. Here I follow Abu-Lughod and Lutz's (1990: 12) suggestions about emotions as 'embodied experiences', i.e. as experiences that involve the whole person, including the body. They suggest that Bourdieu's (1977: 90) concept of 'body hexis' provides ways of thinking about the fact that emotion is embodied without being forced to concede that it must be 'natural' and not shaped by social interaction. Bourdieu

> defines body hexis as a set of body techniques or postures that are learned habits or deeply ingrained dispositions that both reflect and reproduce the social relations that surround and constitute them. The child for instance, learns these habits by reading, via the body rather than the mind's eye, the cultural texts of spaces and of other bodies (Abu-Lughod and Lutz 1990: 12).

By way of example, Abu-Lughod and Lutz (1990: 12) go on to suggest that "rather than thinking, or speaking the respect . . . that helps reproduce a gender hierarchy in Ifaluk atoll in Micronesia, girls follow the curve of their mothers' backs in embodying the bent-over posture of respect". Applied to the case of naptime at Katsura Day-Care Center this conceptualization is illuminating. Through the experience of naptime, it may be suggested, the children learn to embody in themselves the bonds and the sentiments of solidarity and intimacy of the peer group. Rather than explicitly reasoning about these ties, the children learn to 'bear' their relation to the group through the embodied experience of sinking into a 'sea' of their friends. Thus the shifting voice register, the different postures and the distinct smells and physical contact of naptime are the means through which the emotional stance toward the circle of friends is actualized.

But this experience is based upon similar experiences sustained at home. The emotions and sentiments cultivated at the day-care center build on the children's previous 'embodiments' of the close ties and affection found in the home. The center makes use of the fact that the children have already learnt 'how to sleep' with others in a manner that promotes both intimate ties and a feeling of dependency. Learning the comfortableness of resting within the group – despite the difficulties surrounding sleep – is thus based upon the previous experience of learning to feel comfortable enough to sleep at home. Ties with the peer group are thus constructed on the basis of 'pre-prepared' emotions and attitudes. Let me amplify this point further through the relation between sleep and belongingness. Schwartz (1973: 27) suggests the general notion that the component of a person's identity known as 'residence' is based on a definite spatial location, normally the sleeping location. Thus

> a person 'lives' where he sleeps; even more a person *belongs* where he sleeps; sleep establishes where the person is in social as well as spatial terms; it situates him in accordance with membership rather than mere presence and thereby generates an identity for him [emphasis in original].

Thus because belonging encompasses aspects of both cognition and emotion the children are (in one sense) who they sleep with: they are members of their families but also members of their peer group. But notice that there is no choice involved in these identities, because just as the mother–child tie is non-negotiable, so membership in the group is non-negotiable. In this manner, sleeping with peers is part of the way in which the 'naturalness' of group membership is constructed. Once learned these emotions become for the children 'natural' sentiment with a strength of their own. As Denzin (1983: 407) suggests, the 'genuineness' of emotions is rarely questioned: emotional acts have a lived 'realness' that is not doubted. To reiterate, because the learning of emotional stances towards other individuals and towards groups is not explicit, its effects are carried in the body in ways that are *felt* by people to be 'natural'.

A Complementary Explanation

At this juncture, I briefly introduce a number of other interpretations of early childhood education in Japan in order to explain in which way my analysis goes beyond them. Scholars have offered some fascinating answers to the question of how Japanese children learn to shift between the two sets of orientations and behavior found at home and at preschool. Employing what is essentially an educational model, Lewis (1989) suggests that Japanese children gradually master – through being intentionally subject to a complex set of explicit and implicit practices – the new behavioral codes of the preschool. Shields (1989: 5) posits a more general Japanese cultural propensity that is absorbed at preschool: on "all levels, Japanese behavior tends to be highly situational and embraces huge differences in public and private settings". According to him, the children learn to distinguish between what is accepted at home (*uchi*) and outside of it (*soto*) by learning to define each situation as entailing different behaviors and norms. Thus if Lewis' model is one of deliberately teaching knowledge about "new" things once the child has entered preschool, Shields' model suggests that pre-school is the place where children begin to grasp situational ethics.

Rosenberger (1989) suggests a more general model. It should be stated that in her analysis socialization is a peripheral issue, and that rather than talking in developmental terms she is interested in delineating the main contours of a model of the Japanese self. From our point of view, her central notion is the principle of con-textualization (Rosenberger 1989: 99). Her main thesis is that Japanese culture is characterized by a dialectic relationship be-tween four representative modes of expression. She suggests that the development of the ability to shift between modes can be traced to experiences in the lives of Japanese children: along their life course they are subject to contradictory contexts such as family and preschools, elementary and junior high schools, or high schools and university. Her analysis is important both in terms of basing this learned ability to switch modes of expression in the concrete experiences of children and in illuminating the kinds of cultural ideals actualized in different contexts of behavior. But she does not explain how Japanese children internalize these differing modes, nor does she shed light on how the children come to adopt these codes as internally felt motivations. To follow Blacking (1977: 5), what is missing in her analysis is an examination of how feeling adds the dimension of commitment to action.

Jane Bachnik (1992) and Joseph Tobin (1992) take this kind of conceptualization – although not its specific terminology – and apply it more directly to the question of how Japanese children learn to relate to the world beyond their families. In general their thesis centers on how children master the juxtaposition *and* move-ment between the categories of 'home' and 'preschool'. The con-cept crucial to their contention, as I understand it, is *kejime*, the ability – or meta-ability – to make distinctions and to shift in-between contexts and the behaviors appropriate to them (Bachnik 1992: 21). By moving outside the family to preschool, children learn to make these distinctions and thereby learn how to become members of more complex groups. But preschool does this not by offering a world which is totally unlike the world of the home, but instead is a world that is

> simultaneously home (*uchi*) and not-home (*soto*), front (*omote*) and rear (*ura*), a world of both spontaneous human feeling (*honne*) and prescribed formal pretense (*tatemae*) (Tobin 1992: 25)

Their interpretation is thus one of increasing synthesis: children learn through the juxtaposition of the categories of home and preschool to differentiate between them and thus to integrate these two worlds. "*Kejime* can index *how much* discipline, submission of self, or boundedness and conversely, *how little* emotion, self-expression, or spontaneity is appropriate in a given situation" (Bachnik 1992: 11; emphasis in original). To be sure, this explanation is not a static one: first, because it illuminates how the children learn to apply the distinctions between categories of behavior learnt in specific situations later on in other instances; and second, because through the distinction of the paired terms, people do more than 'mirror' the social order. Through "the paired terms social participants are able to *constitute* the very situations that become crucial aspects of the social order" (Bachnik 1992: 22; emphasis in original).

Bachnik and Tobin's proposals appear to be similar to Bourdieu's (1977) notion of how mental structures are learnt through processes of inexplicit learning; learners unconsciously extract from practice a pattern that can be flexibly and innovatively used in new situations (see Strauss 1992: 9). But the problem with all such interpretations is that motivation is not automatically learnt when cultural descriptions or distinctions are learnt. To put this by way of our case, it is not enough to know what cultural information the children are exposed to, we also have to study *how* they internalize it. Let me explain.

While Bachnik and Tobin's thesis (and by extension Rosenberger's proposals) make much sense, I would add that both 'home' and 'preschool' are more than cognitive categories. They are also sets of embodied attitudes and sentiments. The point is that the preschool not only encompasses the attributes of both home and the wider world, but that it also reverberates with and channels the embodied emotions of the family towards the wider world. It is in this manner that we may understand how what is learnt at home and at preschool becomes compelling to the children. The orientation towards the peer group gains its motivational force because it is experiential, it taps into the feelings and desires of the children (Strauss 1992: 13). In this sense, the child's experience at home 'preadapts' (D'Andrade 1992: 37) her or him to internalize certain cultural propositions about the center and the peer group. Commitment to and an internalization of the importance of the group are thus based in concrete life experiences because life experiences are remembered along with the feelings associated with them.

It is for these reasons that the cultural constructs and (meta-) abilities illuminated by such scholars as Rosenberger, Bachnik or Tobin acquire motivational force. By bringing in the experiential dimension of going to preschool – actualized in such activities as naptime – we understand the strength of the ties promoted within peer groups. It is also against this background that we can understand how emotionally laden (and therefore difficult) the movement of children from family into the 'wider world' is, and how the potency of the ties inculcated during preschool is generated.

Organizations, Embodied Experience, and Power

For all of this, emotional postures are not only phenomenologically experienced, nor are they only vehicles for symbolizing and affecting social relations (Abu-Lughod and Lutz 1990: 12). Such postures are also practices that reveal the effects of power. To put this point by way of our case, naptime is not only an embodied experience of groupness, nor is it only a medium for representing the social relations between the sleepers. Sleep also involves the power relations at the day-care center. Along these lines, notice that up to this point I have altogether neglected issues of discipline, and the molding of the children's 'natural' desires and rhythms to those of the day-care center. Here we are led to deal with an issue which is altogether missing from most studies of early childhood education in Japan: the place of power and the *organizational* construction of emotions (see Van Maanen and Kunda 1989: 46).

Berger and Luckmann (1967; 203; see also Turner 1984: 58) propose that socialization does not simply involve the intrinsic problems of learning, because

> the child resists the imposition of the temporal structure of society on the natural temporality of his organism. He resists

eating and sleeping by the clock rather than by the biologically given demands of the organism.

The import of this point is not only that some children resist the patterns imposed at the center, but that from the teachers' point of view these children become "organizational problems". Teachers' responses to these problems reveal both the organizational bases of administering naptime, and how ties with children (and parents) are saturated with power.

On one level, regardless of the caretakers' best intentions as individuals, the center is limited as an organization in its capacity to react to the special needs of children: for instance, allowing more rest to a child who has just returned from holiday or a youngster who went to sleep late the night before. On another level, it is limited in its capacity to deal with something that many psychological studies have documented: the differing propensities of people to sleep at differing times and in various circumstances; for example, catering to 'morning' or 'evening' persons or to youngsters who nap only twenty minutes a day (Lavie 1991). Because preschools (like all formal organizations) are run on the basis of efficient use of resources and the synchronization of individual rhythms to organizational timetables there is little leeway for satisfying individual needs and habits (Ben-Ari, 1995).

Some teachers talked of how the children periodically get 'over-excited' (for instance, after a finger-painting activity) and have trouble falling asleep. A teacher from the group of four year-old children explained more generally:

> We get two or three a year who don't like to sleep or don't sleep at home. We try and put them to sleep but if the problems persist we demand that at least they lie quietly on their *futon* and not disturb the others. We try not to let them go out during naptime to play by themselves in another room.

Such a statement is indicative of how children are controlled not only in the hall where their peers sleep, but also in terms of the lack of choice for alternatives during the rest period. A teacher of the three year-old group related naptime to group life, and thereby sought to legitimate the measures taken to solve 'problems':

> It's not a real difficulty but we have a few children who simply do not like to sleep. It's their personality, and they have problems becoming used to group life. We had two children like this

who entered the group this year in April. They had to get used to falling asleep in the group. But by now [August] they have settled down. It took about two months and we lay down next to them to help them fall asleep.

In such cases, teachers calm and soothe the children in order to adapt them to group life. Moreover, whenever some youngsters create a disturbance during naptime, teachers carefully mobilize their feelings of empathy by telling them to be quiet for the sake of their friends.

Another teacher (in the five year-old group) was most explicit in linking sleeping problems to the different rhythms at home and at the center:

Yes, there are children whose sleeping cycle does not meet the cycle of the day-care center. They play with their parents at home until a late hour, get up late in the morning, and then are not tired by the time we put them to sleep here.

Indeed, while the children are adapting to the order of the center, parents are also being regulated by the teachers. As Fujita (1989) notes, parents are pressured to meet the long-term social ordering goals of such establishments. To be fair, I have recorded only two instances at Katsura *Hoikuen* of direct guidance given to a mother who was having trouble putting her child to sleep at home. But in the interviews I held with teachers, they often mentioned the lack of discipline in and around sleeptime at home. Moreover, at the day-care center our son attended during the early 1980s (Ben-Ari 1987) teachers told parents in no uncertain terms, that by asking for an extension of opening hours they would be shirking their parental responsibility because they would have less time to spend with the children and because they would put them to sleep much later than is healthy.

A related point is that naptime is the period devoted to a host of organizational arrangements like filling out forms, planning activities, holding meetings, preparing teaching materials, or learning songs. These periods are thus important for the smooth running of the center. In this way, just as evening in Western middle-class homes is the opportunity for parents to be by themselves away from the children and to do their own things, so naptime at the center is time for teachers to be by themselves away from the children and to do important (organizational) things. The children thus learn the precedence of organizational arrangements over their individual demands and desires.

But there is yet another aspect of power relations and naptime at the center, one related to gender roles. Tobin, Wu and Davidson (1989: 34) note that in Japan, as elsewhere, the preponderance of women in preschools reveals a persisting link in people's minds between preschool teaching and mothering: "Preschool, although a relatively new institution, thus reflects long-standing values and traditions of sexual inequality and gender-based distributions of labor." From my data it is apparent that sleeping practices tend to replicate Japanese gender roles (Edwards 1989) in two respects: one related to teachers as women, and the other related to the peer group.

On the one hand, although preschool teachers try to minimize sexually stereotyped play among children and to treat the boys and the girls in their charge equally, the absence of male adults in the daily life of the preschool presents children with a world that is female dominated and dissimilar for boys and girls. This situation works towards a replication of wider Japanese conceptions of gender relations within preschool. Paradoxically, the very similarity of home and preschool contributes to the acceptance, by the children, of women's 'natural' roles as centered on caretaking.

On the other hand, because the peer group is a source of knowledge about appropriate behavior, and a framework within which children can socialize each other (Greif 1977: 156), the roles boys and girls undertake are crucial. Thus in helping to put the younger children to sleep the older girls seem to reproduce in themselves both their mothers' *and* their teachers' positions. These girls, it may also be posited, function as (small scale) role models for younger girls. Naptime thus provides one arena for girls to rehearse their role as older adult women (see also Peak 1991a: 82).

The Continuity of Form

If my depiction has certain similarities to portrayals of Japan's much vaunted industrial paternalism, this is not incidental. What one does finds in Japanese preschools is socialization to a certain mix of loyalty, care and discipline and comfortableness in hier- archical groups. The following story may illuminate the continuity between preschools and the workplace.

At the end of my first fieldwork in Japan (between 1981–83) the professor I was assigned to at Osaka University retired. The way in which the students decided to honor his retirement is characteristic of a wider set of phenomena. Each one of us paid a sum of a few thousand Yen, and a group of twenty individuals – students and a few young lecturers, women and men – set off to a hot-springs resort located to the north of Kobe. Upon arrival there, the group separated according to gender and the men and the women entered two communal baths. Afterwards, we again congregated and ate a communal meal which lasted for about six hours. The atmosphere was marked by familiarity and the meal was accompanied by drinks, and constant joking and laughter. At about one in the morning, we decided to go to sleep. *Futon* were taken out of the cupboards and spread out in the middle of the room. Everyone – women and men, students and teachers – lay on their backs and talked, laughed, and dozed. The ambience was marked by a coziness that allowed a large measure of intimacy and for conversation to flow over personal and academic matters. Finally we went to sleep.

Caudill and Plath (1986: 274) observed three decades ago that many Japanese "place great emphasis on collaterality (group inter-relatedness) not only in the family but in many spheres of activity. They also find much of their enjoyment in the simply physical pleasures of bathing, eating and sleeping in the company of others." Lebra (1976: 14) adds that the "body warmth experienced in co-sleeping is likely to be retained in the child's memory and recalled with pleasure after he attains maturity". When one observes contemporary Japan, it becomes readily evident that patterns of co-sleeping – with an emphasis on intimacy and closeness, and a de-emphasis on sexuality – recur in many Japanese organizations. One finds them in a variety of contexts such as the school trips, excursions of village and neighborhood associations (Ben-Ari 1991; 174–5), and most significantly in the overnight outings of work and work-related groups (Matsumoto 1970; Rohlen 1973; 1986; Kondo 1990: 182–88).

What is the significance of the fact that patterns of co-sleeping are found in the framework of Japan's modern industry? In the scholarly literature, much has been made about how contemporary workplaces make use of patterns of behavior and feelings learnt during primary socialization for their own purposes (van Helvoort 1979; Whitehill 1991). Tobin (1992: 31) suggests that a child who has gone through a Japanese preschool "will do well in other contexts in Japanese society, including, for example, in the life of the Japanese company man . . . [Both are] members of an institution that is both home (*uchi*) and not-home (*soto*), and an institution that requires fluid shifts between *omote* and *ura*."

Could I suggest that along the lines of my analysis, co-sleeping – and by extension co-bathing and drinking and eating parties (Ben-Ari 1993) – are 'key scenarios' (Ortner 1973) in Japanese culture. These scenarios are valued because they formulate a culture's basic means-ends relationships in actable forms. They may be formal, usually named events, or sequences of action that are enacted and reenacted according to unarticulated formulae in the normal course of everyday events. My point is that if we conceptualize forms like co-sleeping as certain scenarios that Japanese people learn to 'carry in their heads', we can understand how these scripts can be activated in a variety of contexts throughout their life course.[8] What my interpretation clarifies is the place of accumulated experience (preadaption) in compelling people to carry out these key scenarios: through co-sleeping with his or her peer group during childhood, the adult Japanese has learnt to embody the experience of grouping in an intimate manner.

Conclusion

I began my analysis with the question of how Japanese people add ties and orientations to horizontal groups to the strong dyadic and hierarchical relations nurtured at home. In answering this question I suggested that a focus on naptime in preschools allows us to explore two interrelated issues. The first is naptime as a social form which has its own problems, rules and internal dynamics. Such a conceptualization has allowed us to examine both the organizational management of sleep, and the ways in which nap-time at preschool is related to patterns of putting children to sleep in the home. We found that sleeptime at day-care centers is an occasion through which patterns inculcated at home are subtly used in order to further the goals of preschools. The second issue is the inner experiences of the children within these forms. It is through these experiences that the link between cognition, emotion and motivation is best understood. Without an account of the relation between culture and motivation we may have an intuitive sense that there are culturally based strivings but we have no explanation for how these strivings are internalized and then govern behavior in subsequent situations (D'Andrade 1992: 23). Thus my argument is that naptime is one form through which day-care centers effect the transfer of strong relations from the family dyad to the peer group. There is a transfer here – or an addition – of the warmth, the 'comfortableness, and the commitment and involvement of children in the dyad at home to the wider group. In this manner, the question of 'who sleeps with whom?' (Caudill and Plath 1986) continues to be an important one for Japanese throughout their lives.

My analysis does not imply that there are no individual oriented activities or that individuality is not promoted in Japanese day-care centers. It would be a mistake to see such institutions as efficient organizational machines for creating children (and later adults) that fit smoothly into a variety of groups. What such practices as naptime do imply is the inculcation of certain traits and qualities associated with 'being Japanese'. To be sure, co-sleeping exists in a variety of cultures in such guises as hikes and treks, slumber parties or army barracks and hospital wards. What I have attempted to illuminate is how such practices have been institutionalized within the framework of institutions of early childhood education in contemporary Japan. Along these lines, if naptime is related to patterns of 'becoming Japanese' it must also be understood as one of a range of activities in preschools which I explore in greater detail in the following chapters.

Notes

1 These arrangements are aimed, like those at the center studied by Fujita and Sano (1988: 82–2), at inculcating a sense of responsibility in children by encouraging them to help in the preparation of the rooms for sleep.

2 As Schwartz (1973: 23) says, "the sleep role, like all roles, requires substantial physical and/or mental preparation, cannot be abruptly taken on and cast off; its assumption must be preceded by an institutionalized 'transition phase' wherein the individual may gradually adapt himself to it".

3 Hendry (1986a: 44) for instance, reports that in a survey she carried out (in a kindergarten) out of 176 children only twenty slept in their own room while the rest either slept in the same bedding or in the same room as their mothers.

4 As Dore (1958: 49) explains, beyond "the limits of actual cramped discomfort, crowded sleeping seems to be considered to be more pleasant than isolation in separate rooms. The individual gains a

comforting security and it is a sign that a spirit of happy intimacy pervades the family."

5 It is along these lines that the continued use of tatami floors for infants (see for example Hendry 1986a: 129) and futon for all children in preschools should be seen. Using what are perceived to be quintessentially Japanese equipment is part of the way preschools 'Japanize' the children and compensate for the growing trends of middle-class families to sleep in beds and to provide their children with private bedrooms.

6 In fact, the gradual and gradated process of weaning goes on in all of the day-care centers that I visited. For example, at the center our son attended at the beginning of the 1980s, for the group of older children going to school the following year, naps are steadily reduced from five times down to once a week before being completely eliminated.

7 This situation contrasts with the American center Tobin and his associates studied (1989: 141), where the children – as part of the activities designed to teach how to exercise free choice – sleep in places they individually pick. Indeed, in one ethnography of an American day- care center, sleep is mentioned only in so far as it bears on how children choose what to play with until they rest (Provence *et al.* 1977: 164).

8 Moreover, just as we talk about different actors' or directors' interpretations of a script, so conceptualizing the issue in this way allows us to discuss how issues of gender, power or context come into play in the actualization of such forms or scripts.

Hoikuen, *Kibbutz, and Sleep*

Very often I have been asked, in Israel as well as when I travel abroad, whether the Japanese day-care system is not like the system of childcare found in the Israeli kibbutz (pl. kibbutzim) I like to reply to this question with the following story which underscores both the similarities and the differences between the systems.

I was born on a kibbutz about forty years ago. A few weeks after my birth I was placed – like *all* the children of my age – in a children's home where I lived until my parents left the kibbutz when I was six years old. As was customary in kibbutzim of that period, we lived (that is, ate, slept and played) in the children's home and met our parents every day for a few hours. In the afternoons and at night we were put to sleep collectively: a caretaker tucked us into our individual beds (all placed in one room), read us a story and then retired to an adjacent room where she (more rarely he) rested until we woke up. These arrangements were consonant with the ideology of the kibbutz. Living in a children's home was designed to offset – according to the pre-vailing notions of such settlements – the adverse effects of family units. Based on sound socialist principles, residing together was intended as a means to inculcate among the children a feeling of belonging to the collective and a sense of responsibility to one's peers. We were considered to be the children of the kibbutz as a whole (and in a manner of society as a whole).

At first sight, this depiction may sound rather like the situation that I have described in Japanese day-care centers. But this is only a surface resemblance because the two systems proceed from different assumptions. First, within the confines of the children's bedroom, the actual arrangements for sleep were based on rather conventional Western notions: we all slept in separate beds (i.e. private spaces) which were placed in permanent places. Secondly, by tucking us into bed and then leaving to the adjacent room, the caretakers were trying to inculcate in us a sense of independence, a sentiment of separation from adults. And thirdly, and most importantly, while in the kibbutz the governing notion (at that time) was that the collective is a substitute for the family, in Japan there is an explicit recognition (on the part of experts and parents) of the crucial importance of the family for the normal development of children. Group life (including sleep) is thus seen as an addition to, not as a replacement of, the family unit.

Whenever I have told my 'sleep in the kibbutz' story to Japanese people, their reaction has been a rather incredulous (if not shocked) response. I often sensed that people just stopped short of censoring my mother and the lack of feeling and respon- sibility that she showed by allowing me to be taken from her and placed in a dwelling for youngsters. In a curious way I was led back to these reactions when I read about the responses of Japanese people to the Chinese boarding program studied by Tobin and his associates (1989: 99). The Japanese asked: "How can the Chinese do this to their children?" "Are Chinese parents forced to send their children away by the government?" and "Aren't the Chinese aware of how harmful this sort of round-the-clock institutional care can be to small children, who need the daily love and support of their parents?"

Chapter 4

Learning to 'Group'
Play, Embodiment and Emotions

Introduction

In the previous chapter I focused on the *transition* from home to preschool. I suggested that an analytical framework which takes into account the experience the children undergo may aid us in understanding this moment. In the following two chapters I take both my empirical and theoretical concerns a step further. Theoretically, I explore the manner by which a set of central educational emphases are internalized by the children *within* preschools. Empirically I focus on a variety of structured and unstructured educational and play activities.

Two of the primary educational goals which Japanese preschools work towards achieving – on both ideological and practical levels – are 'group orientation' or 'group consciousness' (*shudan seikatsu, shudan ishiki*) and 'perseverance' or 'persistence' (*gaman, gambaru*). While the first goal is related to the collective activities that take place in preschool, the second is more person or individual centered. Many studies of Japanese preschools have illuminated the variety of practices by which these dominant cultural constructs form part of the explicit and implicit curriculums of such institutions (see Lewis 1989; Hendry 1986a; Peak 1991a; 1991b; Singleton 1989: 11; Kotloff 1988: 42). These studies suggest that such forms as small group activities (*han*), conflict management by peers, cooperative games and play and the use of uniforms and naming customs all work toward inculcating both a sense of groupism and the ability to persevere.

In the next two chapters I argue that while these studies have begun to tackle the theoretical issues involved in understanding how educational goals in Japanese preschools are internalized, they have not gone far enough. Specifically, I contend that the *assumption* in most of these works is that the practices and educational forms found in preschools somehow 'naturally' lead to the inculcation of group orientation and to personal discipline. In many previous studies, I argue, preschool activities are treated as a sort of 'black box' through which the children move only to emerge properly socialized. There is relatively little explicit theoretical treatment of the interpersonal dynamics and individual centered experiences by which the children internalize these twin educational emphases.

In the following chapters I argue that two interrelated theoretical problems are involved in understanding this process of internalization. The first is the manner – the actual mechanisms – by which preschool practices lead to group life and persistence becoming natural, taken for granted parts of the children's lives. The issue here is to show how these twin considerations take on a quality which Geertz (1983) terms the 'of-courseness' of common sense understandings. The second problem is the way these emphases gain 'directive', or motivational force. As Strauss (1992: 10) notes, "motivation is not automatically acquired when cultural descriptions of reality are learned". The point here is to illuminate the manner by which 'grouping' and 'persevering' ac- quire motivational significance for the children.

I explore these issues through a focus on the play and games found at the day-care center. I will move from the structured, intentionally (teacher-) directed activities to the relatively unstructured, ambiguously intended and mostly children-directed activities. The reasons for introducing this wide array of practices are ethnographic and theoretical. Ethnographically, I describe a number of activities that hitherto have not been fully portrayed in the literature on Japanese preschools. Theoretically, I argue that it is only out of experiencing the variety of activities at preschool that the internalization of groupism and perseverance can be understood.

Play and Games

Morning Activities: Organized Exercises

When asked what they will 'do' today, teachers almost invariably answer in terms of the major program arranged for the morning. Such activities are most similar to the ones found in kindergartens (*yoochien*) and figure as the primary 'units' in planning the monthly schedule of the day-care center (Ben-Ari 1995). Let me give four examples of these structured, teacher-directed programs that I have recorded in my fieldnotes.

Art education. As the group of four year-old children entered the hall with its two class teachers and myself, the children were welcomed by the art education teacher (a veteran with twenty years of experience, who advises the center on matters related to her expertise). She invited the youngsters in by greeting them with cries of '*irrashaimase*'. Explaining that this is the word used in welcoming customers to shops and stores, she informed the children that today "we are going to play as though we have a shop here, a shop selling machines". When no one answered her question about what a machine is, she turned to one of the class teachers. The teacher replied that there are many kinds of machines like one in which you press a switch and it makes a wind, a fan. The children then began volunteering responses related to machines they have at home: televisions, videos, vacuum cleaners, and washing machines.

"What we will do today then," continued the art education teacher, "is to make machines. We will make them by pasting things on boxes, and by pasting boxes together." She went on to show the children what she and the teachers had prepared: boxes of various sizes, small plastic caps, straws, metal rings, toothpicks, disposable chopsticks, sellotape, magic markers and scissors. Before beginning she reminded everyone that like a real shop 'we must be careful not to sell out the boxes: please leave the boxes you don't need for your friends".

After these few short moments, the children, who had been anticipating this activity since being told about it during morning assembly, assaulted the boxes. Scattering equipment around them, groups of two to five children began working on individual projects: they sat together and talked occasionally, but worked by themselves. There was almost no intervention by the teachers at this stage, although from time to time they inquired about what the children were making. In most cases, the children – busy cutting, attaching, pasting and coloring – answered that they 'didn't know'. After about thirty minutes no more boxes were left, and the teachers declared the shop 'sold out'. Some of the children had problems in cutting and pasting the rather thick cardboard boxes. Although well aware of these difficulties, the teachers did not intercede, and only helped once a youngster had gone through (what seemed to me to be) an excruciating effort at tackling the problem by herself or himself.

The children then began to name the machines they had pre-pared, and to add additional features (extra switches, for instance) in order to fit what they had designated as cars, ships and refrigerators. Having finished his vehicle, one boy began to drive it around the hall and soon some of the other boys followed him. As I stood and talked to the teachers, many of the children came up to show us what they had made. We then went back to join the children, and I helped them prepare flags (colored pieces of paper attached to chopsticks) of Japan, Israel, and the United States which were attached to the machines. Two children began a fight which quickly degenerated into a kicking match. Unperturbed, one teacher simply asked them to be careful and to 'be considerate of their friends' (*otomodachi ni odaiji ni shimasu*). Finally, after about an hour, the children were told that if they wanted to take their products home, to place them in the class room.

Rhythmics class. I joined the group of oldest youngsters, the five year-old children for their weekly rhythmics class in the hall. The instructor (a professional hired by preschools in this part of Kyoto) led the activity with the full participation of the two class teachers. She welcomed the children and told them that "today we will have fun; we will enjoy ourselves". Sitting at the piano (placed at the side of the hall) this teacher alternated slow and fast rhythms, and had the children walking (using long and short steps) and stopping at different paces. Slowly, she increased the tempo of the fast pieces until the children were running. Then, punctuating the activity with explanations, the children were introduced to more complex tasks: different kinds of hops and sprints, running in place, changing directions, stopping on one foot, and revolving in place. One handicapped boy participated as much as possible by crawling in and around the other members of his class. He was aided by one of the class teachers and occasionally by girls from the class itself.

After about fifteen minutes, the instructor asked the children to sit together. She played a song and asked the children if they knew it. Some answered yes, that it was the 'ants' song' (*arisan no uta*). "That's right, it's a song about an ant that goes shopping. But what do ants like to buy? . . . Yes, sweet things, but like what?." The children shouted back about candy, peaches, and melons. Slowly teaching the song to those children who did not know it, the teacher ended each stanza with an onomatopoeic sound of ants going in different directions: '*chon, chon, chon*'. Then, putting her clenched fists to the top of her head and raising each forefinger, she asked the children if they had heard of 'feelers' or 'antennas' which are like the eyes and ears of ants. This is what the ants do when they look for food, she said, and asked the children to mimic her. The children then sang the song and at the end of each stanza went to different parts of the hall to look for food. The instructor continued: "How many of you are here today? Nineteen. All right then, I want to hear nineteen voices." Because their heads were bent, the children initially collided with each other. But after a few practice runs they seemed to feel where their peers were going and the bumps and bangs were minimal.

In the next activity the children were divided into pairs and skipped and clapped in a coordinated manner according to the music. These exercises were concluded by substituting a hand-to-hand clap, a tap of butt to butt between partners. Finally, to return to the theme of ants, the instructor placed a large red ball – alternately a cherry, a strawberry and a tomato to feed the ants – in the middle of a circle the children had formed. Corresponding to the rhythm of the song, the children passed the ball around, handing it without dropping or bouncing to the person standing next to them. Much care was taken that the children coordinate their actions with each other and with the beat of the music.

Pool activity. Assembling next to the small pool (a plastic basin placed on a small metal frame), the three year-old children began with 'radio exercises' (*rajio taiso*). All of the children seemed to know these drills, and those who did not followed the lead of other children or of the teachers. I then showered the youngsters, while the teachers threw some marbles into the pool. The children were invited to swim (actually to crawl on their hands and knees) and look for the marbles. No competition was held, and no one was given any recognition for finding the greatest number of marbles. Next, the children 'swam' through a hoop, and went through a lap around the pool. One girl declined to participate and a teacher cajoled, persuaded and finally got into the pool with her. Lastly, the children played with soap bubbles next to the pool.

Tate-wari kyooiku. Literally meaning 'vertical education', this term suggests programs that cross age and class groups.[1] On this occasion the children in the older three groups were to go for a picnic to a nearby park, but were prevented from doing so because of heavy rain. As a consequence, the children congregated in the hall for an impromptu, but highly organized set of activities. Led by the deputy head of the center, who always seemed to have an armory of games and activities at her disposal, the children were led through a lively array of actions that flowed one into another.

She began by telling the children that as it had been raining in the past few days and as the children did not have a chance to use the pool, we would turn the hall into a pool. "Let's begin by swimming like frogs", she suggested. Divided into groups that included members of different ages, the children began to 'swim' with those members not participating shouting '*gambare*' ('keep at it', 'stick to it'). At this stage and during every other activity, the teachers participated and shouted along with the children. Next, in their class groupings the children 'swam' across the hall to the waiting teachers, touched their hands and 'swam' back. The three or four handicapped children were helped by the teachers who pulled, pushed, and encouraged them to complete each exercise. Although I noticed no teacher giving any of the children explicit urging to do so, many of the youngsters participated in encouraging the handicapped children as well.

Enjoying themselves thoroughly, the children went on to, in turn, walk on all fours, move on their toes, sit on their bottoms and advance forward, and hold hands in pairs or groups of three and run around the hall. These activities again, were accompanied by loud cries of encouragement to individuals or to everyone 'to give it all you've got!' (*minnasan gambare*).

After about twenty minutes one four year-old girl began to sulk and sit out the ongoing activity which then consisted of slinking like a cat towards the end of the hall and back. One teacher went over to her and gently pushed and pulled her while the other teacher and the children shouted and urged her to finish her part. Delicately placing her hand on the girl's, the teacher helped her touch the outstretched hand of the deputy head and to return to her place. The other teacher came over to her, and very quietly but in front of the girl's eyes clapped her hands in appreciation of the effort involved.

Moving in rapid succession, the following activities included singing songs about trains and mimicking the wheels and sounds of the steam, songs about the body and its various parts, and dancing and skipping in different sized groups. The penultimate activity involved everyone sitting down, and groups of six children invited to leave the hall and to return and guess the changes that the teachers and children had made to their seating location, dress, and use of monitor badges. The final activity involved skipping and dancing around the hall with the bolder students as well as the teachers (and the anthropologist) inviting the more reticent children to join them. One of the children with Down's syndrome fell over, and the two children who were skipping with her fell down purposely to make here feel at ease.

Later, during the few minutes before the pre-meal formalities, the deputy head asked the children to think about what they had done during the morning. Stressing that they had learnt new games and persevered in the activities, the deputy head pointed out that they had played very skillfully (*jozu*) with the children of the other age groups. "Wasn't that", she ended, "a good opportunity to get to know new friends."

Free Play: The Commencement and Termination of the School Day

Free play comprises activities which are either independently initiated by the children or are suggested by the teachers. The latter often lay out various games or equipment at the beginning or the end of the day and the children are free to choose to take part in these or other projects. Typically these activities are of short duration.

As in preschools around the world, projects inside the center include individual reading, reading in groups of up to three individuals, or teacher-led deliveries with the children forming a participative audience. In a like manner, puzzles are completed individually, in small groups, or under the direction of caretakers. Similar activities included paper sewing (of pictures drawn either by the children or by adults), putting beads on wires, painting (for example, of ice cream – which I was asked to taste – or of Hokkaido – where two teachers had gone for a holiday), or playing with toys and equipment. These playthings, I was told, are replaced when teachers feel that the children can handle more complex tasks: for example, they provide puzzles of increasing complexity, beads of varied colors and patterns, or more complicated drawings. Activities directly related to preparation for school were, as in the overwhelming majority of Japanese preschools, very rare. Rather, teachers tended to stress the inculcation of certain basic attitudes towards educational tasks. During free play, for example, children were often allowed to draw in small notebooks (actually about eight or ten pages stapled together) under the condition that they utilize all of the pages. Upon completing one such notebook, a five year-old girl declared that this was 'the end of study' (*'benkyoo no owari'*). These short incidents contain strong element of vicarious preparation for school: the ability to concentrate, learning to systematically fill up every page of the notebook, and keeping the promise of not asking for another notebook until you have completed what one is working on.

Another example of combining diligence and responsibility was the manufacture of paper propellers by attaching toothpicks to straws or chopsticks of varying sizes (the older children did this by themselves while the younger ones were helped by the teachers). In this case, again, the children were invited to participate under the condition that they 'stick to it' until completion. A third example was a game in which three cards had to be matched to form a complete picture with the word of the picture (e.g., ship, sled, peach, grasshopper) in the cursive syllabary (*hiragana*) at the bottom. While involving writing, these occasions seemed to be directed more towards other aims. The children were helped at the beginning by the teachers, but later encouraged to help each other or to match the cards by themselves. Again, the lesson was one about social cooperation and individual ability to concentrate.

The hall was the site of much improvised play. One time, three boys turned some chairs into a train and loudly declared – using voices like train conductors – that the while it will stop at Umeda (Osaka) it will not stop at Katsura (the local station). They negotiated their roles by switching between being passengers, drivers and conductors and integrating other children into their game. Another time, two boys and a girl with Down's syndrome began a shouting match. Shouting nonsense syllables in ever increasing loudness and coordinating their cries, all three collapsed into giggles of enjoyment. The shouting match went on until they started, as part of the game, to push each other. As if to explore the boundaries of the possible, one of the boys pushed the girl until she gave a shout of pain rather than joy. The boy who had pushed her (and had been pushed by her) stopped immediately, and said he was 'sorry' ('*gomen, ne*'). After a few brief moments, they continued the shouting match. A final example of play inside the hall involved an obstacle course that two teachers created about an hour before closing time. They took chairs, mats, some blocks and rods, and two small step ladders, and with the children went through the makeshift obstacle course. To shouts of great merriment and encouragement, the children – including two handicapped youngsters – went through the course time and again at ever increasing speed. At the end, as with all activities, the children were asked to help and clear up.

While relatively small, the grounds outside of the center were (rainy days excluded) the site of constant activities. Here children made mud pies and cookies, rode small tricycles, and played on the slide and Jungle Jim. Partly as a reaction to parental pressure 'to let the children play in nature', partly as the outcome of the initiative of two or three teachers, the children often played with sand, water and mud. Using sticks and pails found at the center, they often created rivers and valleys, and wells and fortresses on the side of the grounds. Other times they made pies and foodstuffs which were promptly sold to the teachers, to myself, or the occasional parent who happened to be nearby.

In contrast to the structured morning programs, all of the games I have been describing here went on simultaneously and with 'permeable' boundaries. Children were free to move into, and out of, any activity under the proviso that they keep to the rules of the action. The picture of these periods was thus of a constant flow of children in and out of games and in and out of the center's building. The intermittent games of 'catch' were the only opportunities during which I saw the use – in *one* activity – of both the inside and outside of the center. Much more usual, was the maintenance of a strict boundary between inside and outside: children had to decide *between* games indoors and out-of-doors.

As in the activities inside, free play always ended with *okatazuke*, cleaning up. The children were asked to put toys and implements away and the teachers cleared up the heavier equipment like the tricycles. While I noticed that everyone seemed to know their role and responsibilities, the teachers told me that at the beginning of the year they invest much time and effort in getting the children to turn such tasks into routines.

At the Intersection of Other Activities

These activities are initiated during those ubiquitous, but little studied, periods between planned segments of the day. While teacher initiated and involved all of the children of a particular class, these activities differ from other teacher-led programs in that they rarely have explicit beginnings and ends and can be stretched or contracted to fit with the time left between or on the way to the next event (see also Fujita and Sano 1988: 83). There are differences between teachers in the preferred mode of using these periods: they range from songs and dances, through stories and role play and all the way to impromptu lessons about nature and reflections about class dynamics. This scope allows teachers to show initiative and to express their interactional style. Let me give a few chosen examples of what went on while we were waiting for other activities.

One afternoon while one of the teachers of the three year-old group and the monitors were preparing the afternoon snack, the other teacher initiated an activity derived from the Montessori method. On the floor she taped a line about 3 meters long. The youngsters, the teacher, and myself, had to walk along the line, holding a monitors' bell without making a noise. On another day, she initiated a 'sumo competition' with the children jumping on one foot from the two sides of the classroom.

While I was waiting with the class of the four year-old children for the morning activity (the hall was being prepared), one of their teachers clustered the youngsters in the classroom and took out a number of sea-shells (as she later told me, she had not planned this ahead of time). Taking them out one by one, she explained and then let the children feel the 'whirlpools' on their side. She then suggested that the children listen to the sound of the sea inside of them. Finally, she proposed that the children smell the shells. When one girl said that they stank, the teacher simply said that this was the smell of the sea. As there was still some time left, she asked the children whether they knew how old the shells were. After listening to the children's various estimates, she told them of the generations that it had taken for the shells to develop. On another occasion, this teacher used a few spare moments we had to talk with the children about the snails and fish in the center's aquarium. Her fellow teacher liked dance much more. During 'in-between' periods she taught the children various songs and types of rhythmic clapping and marching sequences.

Two other activities were common in the groups of older children. The first was the very popular 'paper, scissors and rock' game. Usually this game was used in order to determine the order by which children would, for example, begin a game, or take turns at an activity. During the 'in-between' periods, however, they were accompanied by a song and played just for the fun of it. We played the game just to see who wins and to make the time pass until the next game. Another popular game was to sit in a circle (usually including the teacher and myself) while someone would walk around, place a handkerchief behind another, and then run to her or his place without being caught by the person behind whom the handkerchief had been placed.

Primarily a response to the organizational problem of coordinating the time-space slots of different groups and roles, and to the individual problem (in organizations) of waiting, these 'in-between' activities should not be seen as unimportant. As I presently show they are means to control the children, and to foster a group spirit in them. Here we see play as it is interwoven into the schedule of the *hoikuen*. The governing logic of these activities involves coordination between classes and the need to govern the flow and the possible noise the children could create.

The Aim of Preschools

When I discussed the professional aims of preschools with teachers at Katsura *Hoikuen*, they declared (in ways similar to teachers in other such Japanese institutions) that their primary goal is 'preparing children for life' (*seikatsu*). When I pressed for greater detail they referred to such themes as learning to cooperate in groups or the ability to concentrate and maintain self-discipline. Many of the caretakers in the center mentioned the importance of such 'practical' pursuits as sleep, meals or the rituals of coming and leaving the center in achieving these goals. But it is in the more structured programs dictated by the curriculum that most of them see their professionalism coming into full play. Such programs, to put this somewhat theoretically, are seen by the teachers as contributing to the 'developmental trajectory' of children.

Yet these structured activities are not centered on academic matters. On the one hand, as in other countries (Tobin *et al.* 1988: 195) "preschool staff feel a similar and increasing pressure from parents to prepare children for academic and economic success".

Yet on the other hand, in contrast to these insistences, teachers, educational experts and (*some*) parents stress that the aim of preschools is not and should not be academic preparation in the narrow sense of the word. Rather, "the Japanese de-emphasis on narrowly defined academic subjects in preschool does not reflect a lack of interest in academic readiness; instead it is part of a long-range strategy for promoting children's educational success" (Tobin *et al.* 1988: 191). This long-term strategy is predicated on inculcating in the children a complex set of basic personal skills and attitudes and the ability to cooperate and function in groups. Indeed, even a cursory review of previous studies reveals how these notions can be found in almost all Japanese preschools. Peak (1989: 121) for instance, notes how teachers make a concentrated effort to get youngsters to like coming to preschool. Sano (1989: 137) talks of how teachers stimulate and excite the children, while Lewis (1989) records the emphasis on the enjoyment of the school experience. Finally, DeCoker (1989: 56) quotes one principal who stressed that in her preschool reading, speaking, and listening are emphasized as a basis for future literacy. This point was summed up by one Katsura teacher (this was her fourth year at the center) in reply to my question about preparations for school:

> We don't teach them anything directly. The most important part is to create a kind (*yasashi* lit. gentle) feeling between friends [in the group] (*otomodachi*) and the ability to be independent and to cooperate between themselves. They can learn all of the things related to school once they get there.

But the question that such statements raise is one about the mechanisms by which central educational goals are internalized by the children. In this chapter I deal with the notion of group related matters and in the next with the complex of traits related to personal discipline.

'Groupism': the Experience of Incorporation

A number of characteristics of participation in institutions of early childhood education seem to work towards the promotion of a sense of group identity and membership. Take, for example, Fujita and Sano's (1988: 95–6) suggestions about the assumption on which attendance patterns are based. In Japanese preschools, and Katsura *Hoikuen* is no exception, children can expect to be in the same class with the same children every day for the duration of the whole year. By contrast, in many American and British preschools, children may move 'up' to classes of older youngsters even in the middle of the year according to their birthday. Moreover, in Japan advancement from one age grade up to the next is only done at the end of the year and for the group as a whole.[2] In this respect, the message in Japanese institutions is of membership in some kind of 'permanent' entity which is 'beyond' the individual (and which is created by the organization to which the child belongs).

These assumptions form the background for patterns of actual participation in preschool activities. In the first place, there is a stress on getting all of the children to join both the more formal projects and the 'in-between' events led by teachers. On the basis of my observations, I concur with Peak (1989: 116) who observes that unwillingness to join group activities is particularly "threatening to preschool teachers, who are well socialized members of Japanese group-oriented culture". Along these lines, activities at Katsura were marked by constant efforts on the part of teachers to involve all of the children in group concerns. Teachers often kept a whole class waiting while they persuaded and coaxed recalcitrant youngsters into taking part in activities. Indeed, this kind of effort even went up to the point, as in the case of the reticent girl in the hall, of gently but firmly using their own bodies to 'force' the children to go through the motions of participation.

Similarly, in many group endeavors children undergo a constant shift between the roles of performers and audience. As in the examples of the obstacle course, the rhythmics class and the 'swimming' meet in the hall, children alternate between executing a sequence of actions in front of the other students, and comprising the viewers who look at their fellows. Being an audience involves more than simply waiting their turn, or passively absorbing the basics of performance. Being part of an audience is an *active* role: it involves dynamic participation. Thus, during the rhythmics class and the movement over the obstacle course, peers on the sidelines were performed to, but they also took part in the performance itself by shouting encouragement to the participants, and by suggesting ways for better execution.

These features are complemented by a consistent effort by teachers to downplay competition between individuals and the potential emergence of a ranking according to ability or skill within the group. Thus for instance, both the mini-sumo matches and the race around the obstacle course did not involve any advancement towards a 'final' match or run in which the overall winner would be singled out. Indeed, this kind of behavior is found in a variety of endeavors including the annual sports day. During this annual event, and in the rehearsals leading up to it, the emphasis is on participation *per se* rather than on a specific individual's achievement. Hendry's (1986a: 142; Ben-Ari 1986) comments about such occasions are insightful: "Typically, in the West, sports day is an occasion for the recognition of individual achievement and competitive spirit . . . Not so the Japanese version. Races are held . . . but they almost all involve some kind of cooperation as an integral part of the event, and individuals represent a larger group such as their class."

The stress on participation is reinforced by the expectations and behavior related to free play. Because of the rather loose structure and permeable boundaries of such free play, new members are incorporated fairly easily into what is going on. Yet these patterns of incorporation are illuminating. In the more structured activities some pressure is exerted on recalcitrant children to participate is consistent with the findings of many observers. What I found however, is that a no less consistent pressure is put on children already taking part in free play to let other children join. Thus, if a child wants to enter a 'free' activity, teachers would often gently intervene and suggest that participants let her or him take part.

Next, take the presence and role of teachers. In the structured projects and in the 'in-between' periods, class teachers lead their respective groups. But even during periods of free play the teachers 'grant' their presence by walking around and traversing the various clusters of children. Indeed, according to my notes, during times of free play before the morning assembly, teachers often attempted to 'visit' all of the sites where the children play. A related matter which involves teachers and pupils are the *hanseikai* (meetings for reflection). As Kotloff (1988: 80–1) observes for the preschool she studied, even if the act of reflection – basically an act of seeing oneself from the outside – is focused on an individual matter, the fact that these meetings are held in a group context works towards integrating that person's affairs into the collective life of the classroom. All of the mechanisms that I have just outlined, it could thus be argued, work towards the creation of a group orientation. But things are more complex.

Theoretical Shortcomings: My Own

In order to introduce this complexity, I move onto a more theoretical level. A few years ago I became fascinated with the question of how Japanese people learn 'to group'. I briefly recapitulate my argument in order to delineate its shortcomings and to show how it can be further refined. I suggested, following Gregory Bateson (1972), that such learning is not so much a matter of learning to be a member of a specific group, but rather learning the more general ability 'to group'. I argued (Ben-Ari 1991: 266; emphasis in original) that

> most (middle-class) Japanese acquire through their socialization a learned capacity to move from and relate to a succession of groups throughout their lifetime. This [learned capacity] is related to the complex processes of socialization (direct, anticipatory and vicarious), and to an individual's procession – from childhood to old age – through a whole range of formal and informal groups . . . In rather abstract terms, middle-class Japanese acquire – through a process Bateson (1972: 167) terms deutero- or meta-learning – a capacity to move from one frame (Nakane 1973), *waku* (Plath 1969), or *soo* (Kumon 1982), to another. They learn, then, to relate to groups on a meta-level. That is, they learn to relate to a constant 'idea' or 'construct' of a group although they may move successively or *concurrently* through many concrete or actual groups.

While I will show how this conceptualization does not negate the place of individuals in Japanese culture in the next chapter (Plath 1980), here I continue with the theme of groupism. I based my formulation on Bateson's insight that the form and not only the substance of action may teach us something about social behavior (Schwartzman 1978: 213). His insight centered on the notion that human communication occurs at various levels: that of messages (or contents) and that of metamessages (or contexts). Metacommunicative messages act as 'frames' or 'frameworks' which provide information about how the actual message should be interpreted.[3]

To put this point by way of my case, contexts of curricular projects, 'in-between' periods and free play all carry messages about how to interpret these very activities. In other words, the particular characteristics of class participation, teacher attendance and interplay of performers and audience all transmit quite clear 'notices' to the children that to play or to game is (also) 'to group'. The overall message – even in free play – is 'this is a collective endeavor'. In this way, learning how to participate in a game, to take part in free play, or to join in a structured activity is to grasp how 'to group'.

Furthermore, following Catherine Bateson (1991: 114), once internalized, these orientations become self-validating. Children exposed to 'grouping' over time learn to group. Faced by a new situation, they proceed under the assumption that the proper way to act is to cooperate, take others into consideration, and be identified and committed to the new social framework. The point is that these self-validating premises are learnt and maintained throughout one's lifetime so that they form a set of unquestioned assumptions shared by members of Japanese (middle-class) culture and permeating their experiences.

Such a conceptualization lets us understand that it is the constant set of messages *across* a variety of preschool situations that gives the children the set of shared assumptions about grouping. This point may be better understood against the background of the contrast Tobin and his associates (1989: 106–7) draw:

> Chinese notions of the group are inextricably linked to the concept of order. A disorderly collection of children is not a group. To the Japanese, in contrast, groups can be chaotic as well as orderly, spontaneous as well as structured, anarchic as well as prosocial. Children doing morning exercises are a group, but so are children playing wildly in the courtyard after lunch; quality-control circles in a factory are groups, but so are five or six workers going out together to a bar after work.

Japanese children thus learn that 'grouping' involves an assortment of structured as well as fluid contexts. 'Groupism' according to this formulation then, is more than an inculcated attitude towards membership in a fixed social entity. Rather, it involves the ability to cooperate in, to coordinate one's actions with, and to feel comfortable in the framework of a *variety* of collective situations.

Along these lines, I contend that 'grouping' is one 'key scenario' (Ortner 1973) or, better still, central 'schema' or 'model' (D'Andrade 1992: 29) in Japanese society. Conceptualizing the process as one in which the children learn the 'schema' of groupism allows us to understand the generative aspect of this knowledge – the learning of the *ability* to group. Once mastered, the schema of grouping can be applied – not automatically but creatively – to new situations during preschool or later throughout the children's lives.[4]

But I would argue that such a conceptualization is still not enough. To take off from Blacking's (1977: 4) critique, in conceptualizing the matter as one of learning a schema of (group) action, my analysis, like many studies of Japanese preschools, proceeds from a simple assumption: namely, that the more the children associate with each other in different preschool contexts the more they will care for and identify with each other, and the more they will learn to collaborate in group settings. But discussing cultural or behavioral salience is not enough. As Strauss (1992: 13) aptly puts it, "What can we say about the reasons why some cultural constructs, but not others acquire motivational force? . . . [what] types of experience lead people to feel (often without thinking about it much) that a certain course of action is their only reasonable alternative?."[5] The reasons for certain cultural models acquiring motivational force seem to lie in the experiential basis of learning. The crucial link is emotive in nature:

> life experiences are remembered along with *feelings* about them
> . . . [S]elf concepts are acquired slowly over the course of
> development as learned social ideologies about what is right and
> natural for people like oneself are linked to and energized by
> memories of powerful life experiences (Strauss 1992: 14; emphasis in original).

The analytical challenge thus becomes one of understanding *how* the life experiences of children are related to the cultural construct of 'grouping' so that this schema both becomes a 'natural' way of relating to others and is linked to the motivational basis of action. Let us deal with each of these elements in turn.

The (Natural) Embodiment of Thought-Feeling

As I proposed in the previous chapter, Bourdieu's thoughts on 'body hexis' are suggestive in regard to how certain perspectives toward the world become taken for granted. His suggestions provide ways of thinking about how such perspectives are embodied without being forced to concede that they must be 'natural' rather than shaped by social interaction (see Abu-Lughod and Lutz 1990: 12). He defines 'body hexis' as a set of body techniques or postures that are learned habits or deeply ingrained dispositions that both reflect and reproduce the social relations that surround and constitute them. The child for instance, learns these habits by reading, via the body rather than the mind's eye, the cultural texts of spaces and of other bodies (Bourdieu 1977: 90; Abu-Lughod and Lutz 1990: 12).

The underlying mechanisms by which these body techniques are learnt are what Csordas – building upon the works of Merleau-Ponty and Bourdieu – terms 'somatic modes of attention', "those culturally elaborated ways of attending to and with one's body in surroundings that include the embodied presence of others" (Csordas 1993: 138). A good way to understand this term is the 'effort' involved in sight:

> [W]e less often conceptualize visual attention as a 'turning toward' than as a disembodied, beam-like 'gaze'. We tend to think of it as a cognitive function rather than as a bodily engagement. A notion of somatic mode of attention broadens the field in which we can look for phenomena of perception and attention, and suggests that attending to one's body can tell us something about the world and others who surround us . . . Attending to others' *bodily movements* is even more clearcut in cases of dancing, making love, playing team sports, and in the uncanny sense of presence over one's shoulder. In all of these, there is a somatic mode of attention to the position and movement of other's bodies (Csordas 1993: 138–9 emphasis in original).

What does this imply for grouping in Japanese preschools? The first implication is that it is primarily in preschool that children learn – or better still, internalize – the *practices* of attending to the bodies of others in ways that become 'natural'. These practices involve for example, 'attending to' others when sitting down without being in someone's way, lining up and waiting, taking turns in being performers and audience and entering and leaving episodes of free play. Over time at the center, the children begin to share with their peers a set of bodily dispositions – like bowing, sitting, walking, or dancing – in what Csordas (1993: 147) terms a sort of sensory intuition.

But, following Csordas (1993: 147), while labelling groupism a form of 'embodied knowledge' may sound provocative, it is still not enough. We still need to capture the *intersubjective nature* of this kind of knowledge. The postures the children adopt may be a fruitful way to explore these issues. Connerton (1989: 73) observes that postural behavior may be very highly structured and completely predictable even though it is neither verbalized nor consciously taught. While Connerton (1989; see also Abu-Lughod and Lutz 1990) goes on to link posture to a 'choreography' of authority, I would take his suggestions and talk of a 'choreography' of groupism. My point is that the children learn a range of (often implicit and predictable) postural repertoires for attending to their peers.

Let me furnish four concrete examples. The first is the sitting posture involved in the semi-circle the children often create around teachers. While such a stance entails for each child a directed gaze towards the teacher, it also necessitates attending to her or his friends. This attention includes coordinating one's voice and movements with them, getting used the smell of their bodies and breath, not entering their private spaces, and managing the grazing of elbows, knees or other parts of the body with them. What seems to be involved in such actions is an operative or active (but not fully conscious) element of body manipulation.[6] No less importantly, such a seemingly simple act as sitting in a group involves a large measure of self-control. In this way, the subordination of personal goals involved in grouping is learnt through practices of regulating the body.

The second example is the orchestration needed in order to make space for friends while sitting or standing in line. In these cases, the children learn to manage the addition of another youngster by both moving their own bodies and tending to the presence of another's body. Thus whenever I sat with the children (in front of a teacher) they seemed to 'naturally' form a semi-circle around me; as though to integrate me into their midst. Here the acceptance of an individual by the group is actualized through implicit movement in reaction to the impingement of that individual's physical presence. Reaction, however, may be too strong a word, for it implies intention and consciousness. Perhaps reflex – in the sense of an almost automatic action – better captures the sense of such responses.

A third example are the gestures involved in signaling that one wants to enter an episode of free play. During fieldwork, I witnessed time and again how children would adopt a posture of appeal while standing at the side-lines of some game. They would tilt their heads slightly forward, focus their gaze on the playing children, and try to initiate eye contact with them. The playing children would often respond to this supplication by opening up their on-going activity to the new participant. In such cases the body 'holds' the supplication in a way that others cannot disregard.

The fourth example, of which I have many records, is the coordinated use of voices in songs and during greeting sequences. When I or other visitors were introduced to classes, the teachers often made the children say 'good morning' or 'hello' a number of times. Similarly at the end of an activity organized by one of the student teachers the children said 'thank you' collectively. Over time, the youngsters learn how to match the right pitch of their voices, the time or length of the statement and the appropriate degrees of bending the body in a bowing motion that accompanied these greetings and acknowledgements.

These examples illuminate how learning to group involves something beyond both individual intentions and conscious reflection and beyond a specific individual's body practices. That the children carry their bodies in these ways without the need for constant and explicit supervision is related to what Bourdieu (see Csordas 1993: 137) calls the habitus, "an unself-conscious orchestration of practices". Thus sitting in a group, making space for a fellow student and signalling the desire to enter a game are all actualizations of the interpersonal coordination of body practices involved in grouping.

Once internalized, these practices are used by the children naturally and 'automatically'. Our bodies keep the past in an "entirely effective form in their continuing ability to perform certain skilled actions. We may not remember how or when we first learned to swim, but we can keep on swimming successfully . . . without any representational activity on our part" (Connerton 1989: 72). Similarly, the children learn to group without really remembering how they learnt to. Just as there are ways that working at machine or at a desk reinforces a set of postural behaviors which we come to regard as 'belonging' to the factory worker or the sedentary white-collar worker so there are ways in which participating in Japanese preschools (as in such institutions around the world) support patterns of carriage of the body related to grouping. Indeed, "Posture and movements which are habit memories become sedimented into bodily conformation" (Connerton 1989: 94). Groupism recedes into automaticity once learned.

Motivation: Role-Models, Engagement and Choice

For all of this, such practices are more than natural dispositions. They come to carry, via the powerful experiences of preschools, motivational force. To be sure, sets of positive and negative reinforcements figure in the way the children learn the body techniques I have been talking about. But I would ask the reader to keep in mind that the notion of 'reinforcements' is both too predictable – in assuming a specific response for each stimulus – and intentional – in the sense of a conscious monitoring of the reinforcing behavior. Perhaps a better conceptualization would take into account of both the leeway for individual differences within learnt dispositions, and the implicit and at times unintended (but no less powerful) ways in which they are learnt. Accordingly, I suggest a number of ways in which body practices are linked to motivation: identification with significant others – teachers and peers – as role models; creating an experience of engagement with different groups; and the contextualization and differentiation of positive and negative emotions in concrete situations.

As I showed in the previous chapter, the children's connection with, and trust in, teachers is the result of transferring such sentiments from their mothers to the caretakers and of the latters' position as organizational authority figures. While teachers see over-reliance on them as a negative quality, they nevertheless are very conscious of the children's attachment to them and as a consequence the importance of being role models. They consciously set examples of body practices such as sitting and standing, making room for others, and creating a sense of comfortableness in groups. The children for their part, because they 'want to be like the teachers' often copy their demeanor. Thus I often saw situations in which teachers would sit quietly and with their bodies upright in the middle of a group of noisy individuals and simply wait for the class members to copy them. On other occasions they would publicly hand over equipment to a child in an exaggerated manner without directly saying anything about the cooperation this entails but with the clear intent of getting the message across to the children.

The gradual shift of identification and dependence from teachers to the peer group which is part of the implicit agenda of preschools works in a similar way. The arrival of three new children to the center during my fieldwork proved a valuable lesson in this regard.

Their new peers taught them how to sit, how to wait, how to line-up, and how to fulfill the role of audience for others in a variety of implicit ways. Katsura *Hoikuen* of course, is no exception in this respect. As Peak (1991a: 113; see also Kotloff 1988: 80ff) notes, *new* students "are expected to absorb rituals and symbols of group membership such as singing the school song, through observation. In the process of watching, a strong desire to join the group arises, and children develop understanding of their future role".

A closely related point is the positive engagement that teachers try to create in group activities by linking powerful emotions – enjoyment, satisfaction and amusement – to collective activities. Many periods of structured and unstructured activities are marked by what Csikszentmihalyi (1975) has termed the 'flow' experience: the unique sense of focused attention on particular tasks (mountain climbing, car-racing, or even chess, for instance) in which one's skills and abilities are stretched and tested to their maximum. During such occasions, time seems to 'stand still' and all of an individual's attention is concentrated on the task at hand. While the flow experience has been most closely associated with solitary pursuits, I would add that, as in teams sports it may also be found in group situations. Thus for instance, running and dancing together as in the rhythmics class, making each other laugh, shouting suggestions and getting immediate reactions are all aspects of entering this highly enjoyable and sought after flow experience. Like more solitary pursuits, so in these activities, individuals are somehow caught up in something beyond them in which coordination with others – via the collective enterprise of coordinating mental and physical tasks – is central. In this way, flowing implies not only learning to lose oneself in an activity but to lose oneself in a group. It is in this sense, as I understand it, that Blacking (1977: 4) observes that "[t]echniques of the body are not entirely learnt *from* others so much as discovered through others".

On another level however, choice – especially in regard to free play – is also an important element in creating a constructive and secure engagement with the group. The choice the children have in moving in and out of various games and episodes of play works toward creating a positive attitude towards group participation. This feeling of (relative) freedom – the awareness that one can make choices with relatively few constraints – forms a link to motivation because it connects the positive experiences that the children undergo to the schema of grouping. More generally then, it is the choice in free play, the enjoyment of more structured events, and the experience of 'flow' (in both types of activities) which link the schema of grouping to powerful and motivating emotions. In this sense Tobin's insight (Tobin *et al.* 1989: 106–7) is crucial, for it is the *variety* of grouping contexts, and the variety of emotions linked to such grouping, which grants the schema its strength.

Verbalization: Differentiation and Reflection

Yet one more dimension should be brought into the discussion: the role of verbalization in producing the motivation for grouping. My contention is that through a variety of cues, especially (but not only) verbal ones, proper feelings towards one peers are contextualized and labelled so that existing motives are reinforced and elucidated. Take statements like 'wasn't that enjoyable?' (*tanoshikatta ne?*) or 'that was nice!' (*yokatta*). Such declarations link the emotions the children sense to the specific group contexts in which they occur or have occurred. Similarly, expressions like 'what would you feel if you were hit' or 'your friends will be grateful if we whisper so as not to disturb them' work towards marking emotions related to consideration of others. The point is not one of "calling up some prepared emotions, but consists, rather,of helping the child contextualize initially undifferentiated feelings into highly differentiated social situations that give these feelings their affective signature" (Bruner 1986: 116).

But there is more to contextualization than 'helping' children to differentiate their emotions. To take off from Lutz (1987: 301), by saying that I have enjoyed or am enjoying myself, I may, in fact, be producing a motive, or more likely deepen and clarify an existing motive. In this way, the children's understanding of motives and of emotions is enabled or enhanced by social discourse: "in hearing what we ourselves and others say about emotions, we come to understand better (or create) our goals and other perceptions" (Lutz 1987: 301).

Take the case in which the three year-old boy said 'sorry' for hitting the girl with Down's syndrome. Being faced with a situation in which one feels one has wronged someone produces a sense of guilt. But the sense of guilt is only understandable or recognizable by the person who feels it because it is related to 'wronging'.

Neither the phenomenon of *wronging* nor its affective counterpart of *guilt* could occur were it not for the constitutive power of speech to create social reality (see Bruner 1986: 114). In other words, in saying 'sorry' – *with* the accompanying bowing, slight flush of the face, and vague sense of discomfort – the boy learns to contextualize a certain attitude toward another group member.

Finally, take the most explicit episodes of verbalization: the *hanseikai*. In these periods both the natural taken for granted dimension of grouping and the link of grouping to motivation may become 'objects' for deliberation and discussion. On the one hand, just like sports coaches working with athletes in improving performance, so *hanseikai* are used by teachers to comment and elaborate on ways to improve performance in (and of) groups. Children can be given fuller explanations about what the situation is about and what is expected of them. On the other hand, the children themselves are to a great extent active participants in creating groupishness by reflecting about it. By turning episodes of grouping in which they participate into 'social objects' they can criticize, scrutinize and discuss ways of improving patterns of grouping.

Conclusion

I began with a question of how the 'thought-feelings' (Wikan 1989; 1991) of 'groupism' were internalized by children in Japanese preschools. The challenge in examining the process of internalization is one of showing how grouping is both turned into a natural taken for granted attitude to the world and is endowed with motivational force. I argue that it is not enough to say that 'action is culturally constituted', 'the self is culturally constituted' or 'emotion is culturally constituted' because such statements posit causal links ('x constitutes y') without specifying any kind of mechanism or process by which x and y might be connected (D'Andrade 1992: 41). In this chapter I suggested a number of such mechanisms which work through the experiences the children undergo in preschool.

On the one hand, the notion of embodiment – and especially the *intersubjective* element involved in body practices – captures the processes of how group life (or ways of attending to groups) become transparent dispositions to the children. These body practices are what Connerton (1989: 102) terms 'incorporating practices', those largely traceless – in the sense of not providing evidence of their origin – patterns which are remembered by the body. Indeed, given that "every group will entrust to bodily automatisms the values and categories which they are most anxious to conserve" (Connerton 1989: 102) it is not surprising that group related actions are so central in Japanese preschools. Along these lines, understanding how children acquire a sense of and ability to group is only possible in terms of those largely ephemeral and highly situation specific actions through which these practices are incorporated into the body.

On the other hand, by helping the children to differentiate their emotions and 'affix' them to specific situations and meanings, teachers work towards endowing the schema of grouping with motivational force. To be sure, there are biologically based linkages between emotion, arousal and drive on the one side, and learning, problem solving and thinking on the other (Bruner 1986: 113). But what my analysis illuminates is how symbolic activity enters the scene. Thus a discourse on emotions both contextualizes and constitutes the motivational link between (a variety of) group situations and the emotions the children experience in these circumstances.

It is only out of the total experience of preschool that groupism emerges. Participation in structured activities, in 'in-between' episodes and in free play all work together to create the body practices and the motivations associated with groups. We must not be misled into unreflectingly accepting teachers' (that is, 'experts') definitions of what are the most important and serious – 'developmentally relevant' – activities. As we saw, free play and in-between activities, waiting in line and making space for others, opening up a game to new participants and talking about enjoyment are all significant in this respect.

Finally, as I suggested in the previous chapter, it is important to note that emotional experiences do not always involve joy and intense and heightened emotions. To put this by way of my case, groupism is also the everyday, mundane (and often frustrating and boring) existence in collectivities: it is 'lived experience' which is something different from 'emotional experience' and combines both the 'dreary' and the 'intensely meaningful' (Wikan 1991: 291). In the next chapter I turn to a complementary set of educational goals – what I term the *gambaru* complex – which is both more individual centered and deals more directly with the emotions of discomfort, boredom and frustration.

Notes

1 In the past few years this has been very much an 'in' slogan among parents, teachers and some educational specialists in Japan. I even spent a day at a center that is said to specialize in such educational activities and thus to be 'very progressive'.

2 A related matter about which I can only offer my impressions is the Japanese assumption that one attends preschool on all school days. It is thus relatively rare to find, as one does in America, that parents and children take certain days off during the year.

3 To give an example, the statement 'the cat is on the mat' may on the denotative level be an answer to the question 'is the cat on the mat?'. But it may also contain a command or a stimulus that urges the recipient of the message to pick up the cat, kick it, feed it, etc. Alternatively, telling someone where to find the cat may be said in a friendly tone and thus is a communication about the relationship between the communicators (see Schwartzman 1978: 215).

4 Another advantage of using this formulation is that because schemas are hierarchical one can understand how schemas for more concrete activities such as rhythmics, singing a collective song, or going through morning exercises are together related to the more general schema of grouping.

5 Strauss (1992: 13) goes on to suggest that in current cognitive models, "*semantic information* (eg what love is) is not stored in anything like a dictionary, separate from *episodic information* (eg specific experiences of loving and being loved or not loved, reading and hearing about love etc.) (emphasis in original)".

6 I noticed an illuminating example of this point in the groups of two and three year-old children. The teachers often straightened the youngsters' limbs or placed their hands on their knees so that they would not touch others, or 'wander' off into the personal space of friends.

Interlude II

Three Little (Japanese) Pigs

In the popular version in England the first two little pigs, who built their houses of straw and wood, are eaten up by the wolf, who is finally outwitted by the clever third little pig who not only builds his house of bricks, which thus withstands the huffing and puffing of the wolf, but also entices single-handed his predator down the chimney to his death in the cooking pot. The same end meets the wolf in the Japanese version, but not until the first two little pigs have escaped from their flimsy homes to join and cooperate with the third little pig in his effort to catch the wolf. The three then live happily ever after. Even this modification did not satisfy some four year-olds who were watching a hand-puppet play of the story at their day nursery. As soon as the mother pig sent her charges down the road to fend for themselves, a couple of smart boys at the back began calling 'why don't you build a house together? It's much better to cooperate, you know!' (Hendry 1986a: 132–3).

Chapter 5

A Note on the Gambaru *Complex*

Introduction

A host of scholars (White 1987; Singleton 1989; Kotloff 1988: 129ff; Amanuma 1987; McVeigh 1991) have pointed out that in the prevailing Japanese view learning to persevere – *gambaru* – is a key to character development. In this chapter I analyze the ways in which the native cultural model or schema of *gambaru* is inculcated in preschools. Continuing the line of reasoning pursued in the previous chapter, I focus on how this key scenario is internalized by means of a set of bodily and behavioral practices. I argue that *gambaru* is related both to an individual centered cultivation of personal qualities and by way of these qualities to the construction of groups. Empirically, I continue my focus on the variety of games and play activities that I described in the previous chapter.

What is this *gambaru* 'complex'? Singleton (1989: 9) suggests that a good way of understanding both its content and importance is through the notion of an 'unintentional' or 'hidden curriculum' – what anthropologists call a 'cultural theory of learning' – which undergirds more formal and explicit educational programs. Literally *gambaru* means "to persist", "to hang on", or "to do one's best", and the imperative form, *gambare*, is used among members of a group to encourage each other in cooperative activities (Singleton 1989: 10). In reality, *gambaru* is a component of a set of cultural terms loosely centered on notions of *seishin kyooiku* (spiritual education) and which include *gaman* (patience, tolerance), *kuroo* (hardships, difficulties), *enryo* (self-control or discipline) and *shinboo* (patience, endurance) (Moeran 1986: 70; Kondo 1990: chap 3; Gerbert 1993: 172). The underlying notion is that of the tenacity involved in "having the patience and endurance to finish things, the persistence to keep trying in the face of apparent failure, and the general ability to try as hard as possible in whatever one does" (Hendry 1986a: 83–4). Contrasting the Japanese emphasis on *gambaru* with the American stress on ability (that is, IQ and talent) Singleton (1989: 11) contends that in Japan persistence is seen as the secret to educational achievement. Accordingly, because effort is the explanation for success it forms the hidden curriculum in Japanese educational institutions.

Identifying the implicit goals of educational institutions is not enough because there still remains the problem of how these goals are internalized as a set of attitudes and motivations. Japanese educational institutions see direct experience as the most powerful educational strategy in inculcating *gambaru*: carefully constructed experience is more powerful, it is thought, than lecturing or telling (Singleton 1989: 12). But what is it about direct experience that allows the children to internalize such attitudes? What is it exactly, that the children internalize? And, how is arousal related to motivation? My thesis is that the abilities associated with *gambaru* are learnt in Japanese preschools through an intentional set of practices and explicitly related to a motivationally relevant discourse about perseverance and groupism.

The Activities: Internalizing Body Attitudes

Whether through explicit verbal designation or implicit signalling, elements of the *gambaru* complex appear in a variety of activities held at the center. There seem to be two interrelated modes of 'persisting': a more passive set of techniques for controlling the body in relatively static positions, and a more active class of behavior involved in completing tasks by overcoming obstacles.

Sitting and standing are illuminating examples of the passive body control required to master urges, physical discomfort and distractions. In many activities children were told to adopt the sitting style in which their legs are tucked under the thighs in a way that is reminiscent of the posture adopted for Zen meditation, the tea ceremony, calligraphy, or playing traditional Japanese musical instruments. At Katsura *Hoikuen* this posture – termed *okaasan suwari* (literally mother sitting, or squat) – is often used during morning assemblies, when listening to teachers' instructions about programs, and when waiting for one's turn in games that take place on the floor level. More rarely it is used as a disciplinary tactic (making children concentrate on their sitting position and thus stopping them from being a hindrance).[1] In a related manner, children were constantly told not to fidget or wander off while waiting in line and to 'stand properly'. These exhortations were most evident during the 'in-between' periods during which irritation and boredom were coupled with anticipation for the next activity.[2]

That keeping to such sitting and (to a slightly lesser degree) standing positions were difficult for the children was evident from their twitching and squirming, their constant change of body and limb positions, and (sometimes) by their difficulties in getting up. Moreover, teachers' complaints that today mothers do not teach their children how to sit in this 'traditional way' were an indirect indicator of how exacting this squat is for the youngsters. The effort in these situations includes both overcoming the physical pain and discomfort of the posture *and* paying heed to the activity at hand (like listening to teachers' explanations or watching peers). The long-term effect of learning to sit (or stand) without fidgeting is thus the ability to master physical discomfort and attend to something that is beyond the individual. Yet calling this manner of persistence 'passive' does not capture the full quality of the struggle involved. The teachers' exhortations to 'sit properly' (*chantoo suwari*) evoke not only a directive to sit 'correctly' but also to do so in what can be translated into English as 'sprucely'. My point is that for the children even the simple act of sitting in this manner (as many visitors to Japan would attest to) implies not only a submissive conformity but also a more active exertion, a struggle with one's body.

One afternoon, when the class of three year-old children were preparing to go home, I was given another very typical example of the active self-control entailed by perseverance. The teacher was reading out the names of the next day's monitors when one of the girls asked to go to the toilet. The teacher asked her twice whether she 'couldn't bear with it?' (*gamman dekinai no?*) and 'it would be nice if you could bear with it' (*gamman sitara . . .*). The girl answered that she had been trying to wait, and the teacher then let her go. In this instance *gambaru* is focused directly on one of the most crucial body functions, the ability to control one's bladder and bowel movements. One need not require deep psychological insight to appreciate the link that such episodes effect between the cultural schema of *gambaru* and a central set of body practices.

That self-control is not only self-restraint but a more animated achievement of tasks is apparent during play and games that children pursue as individuals. For instance, during free play once the children have chosen a short assignment (for instance, paper weaving, pasting or coloring) they are clearly directed to complete it. The significance of this directive to conclude the assignment in a 'tidy and precise manner' (*kichin to*) is related to inculcating the ability to persevere despite the difficulties the children experience such as coordinating their limbs, or simply being bored. Gaining self-control when crying or griping during physical games is a closely related element. For example, before running the obstacle course I described in the previous chapter (and before participating in other activities like musical chairs) the children had to promise not to moan or whimper if they fell or failed. Moreover, after these exercises, teachers, in a manner we shall return to shortly, often commented on how the group or specific children had persisted in the exercises without complaining or weeping.

It is in its intersubjective nature that the full richness of *gambaru* as a cultural notion is most evident. In this case, *gambaru* involves overcoming desire and body resistance but in ways that are directly related to other individuals: when others are playing or otherwise engaged, an individual has to exercise self-restraint so as not to infringe or impinge on them. This self-restraint, or *enryo*, involves showing a restrained self-presentation and due consideration for other people. But the point is that *enryo* can only be learnt in group contexts: attending to and mastering body sensations is minding and subduing the body's sensations *within* the world of others. "Attention *to* a bodily sensation can thus become a mode of attending to the intersubjective milieu that gives rise to that sensation. Thus one is paying attention *with* one's body" (Csordas 1993: 138).

To get back to the notion of 'grouping' introduced in the previous chapter, we may now understand the significance of such a seemingly simple act as sitting in a group and the large measure of self-control it entails. Peak (1989: 94), with considerable insight, notes that as "a participant in *shuudan seikatsu*, children must learn that their own desires and goals are secondary to those of the group". My point is that the subordination of personal goals is learnt through the necessity of regulating the body. Thus sitting in a group is both an example and an actualization of grouping. It is in this light that admonishments to 'keep to it and be quiet' (*gamman site*) when waking up so that peers who are still sleeping will not be disturbed should be seen. Self-control is explicitly related to consideration for others and to membership in a group.

The perspective I have been offering here helps us understand how *gambaru* – and the associated notions of *gaman*, and *enryo* – as a set of practices become natural to the children. As in the case of 'grouping, so here the children learn to embody these attitudes towards themselves and toward others as a sort of second nature.

Links to Motivation

Internalization entails a set of processes by which socializing agents link cultural models to pervasive and affectively laden rewards and punishments. Given the dynamics of preschools, the role of teachers and peers is of central import in this respect.

Let me begin with the short daily activities which occur during free play. During these events, teachers (and to a lesser extent peers) withhold recognition and support if they think that the children have not made a sincere effort to complete the task despite the difficulties involved. Peak (1987: 112) found that in the kindergarten she studied teachers "usually provide active assistance only after the child has honestly attempted to perform the task himself, or has been made to wait an extremely long time for the teacher's help". So at Katsura, short projects like pasting, coloring, or making puzzles are designed in a way that forces the child to make an effort only at the end of which they receive full notice and acknowledgment of their efforts. The teacher would often stand or sit by the youngster and wait patiently for her or him to struggle with the assignment. Only after the child has made a concerted effort will the teacher provide smiles or words of recognition.

I witnessed other fascinating examples. One afternoon the group of five year old children were tidying the hall. One girl constantly wobbled and fell while picking up the mats and attempting to put them in the cupboards. The teacher waited or did other things while keeping an eye on her. When the group had completed its tasks she complimented the girl, 'Well done!' (*yoku gambatta*) in front of her peers. In the group of four year-old children, one caretaker instituted a system by which the children would paste a small animal figure on a daily table if they had successfully completed their morning exercises. At the end of the month each youngster would receive her or his table and show it to other teachers, to their peers and to parents and grandparents. Here the table functioned as a concrete indicator of how a child had persevered over the course of a month.

In the case of larger scale, more collective events, what is crucial to the creation of motivation is the *interplay* of individual effort and group support. Take the cases of the obstacle course and the 'swimming' meet in the hall. These events begin with the creation of feelings of anticipation by the teachers who say things like, 'today we will be doing something interesting, or 'do you think you can do it?'. In the events themselves, while teachers and peers provide support and encouragement, the emphasis is on individual exertion and effort. Much like the marathon described by Kondo (1990: 100–2) the children did not race against each other as much as against themselves. In this way shouts of 'stick to it' or 'keep at it' (*gambare* or *gambatte*) during the races, or 'well done' (*yoku gambatta*) and 'skillfully played' (*jozu datta*) after the contest offer a recognition of the individual effort involved. In this way a child's sense of accomplishment is heightened by others.

I would posit that in such events the dynamic is much like that found in sporting meets. Cheers of the crowd provide athletes with a 'rush' that is felt bodily and a sense of support which reinforces the continuing effort. At the end of the sporting event, the appreciation and acceptance by the crowd is coupled with the personal sense of achievement (and the gradual relaxation of the body). In a similar way, during preschool games the backing and support that an individual receives from teachers and peers is directly linked to her or his efforts. Afterwards the children may feel both a surge of gratitude towards the others for the support they received and a sense of self-satisfaction at completing the event.

In all of these cases – the more solitary as well as the more collective pursuits – a crucial condition is that the task have some chance of meeting with success. That is, the experience will come to have motivational force only if the individual has a likelihood of meeting with success. The trick (as all preschool teachers know) is to place the tasks at a level which will not frustrate the children because it is too difficult or bore them because it is too easy. Thus for example, when the teachers saw that the obstacle course they had originally constructed was too difficult for the three year-old children they changed the layout to fit their capabilities. On another occasion I saw a teacher delicately manage a game of putting balls into holes of different sizes and colors so that the children seemed to reach the edge of frustration. She later explained that such experiences will make the children learn the benefits of 'perseverance' (*gamman*).

Here again, talk about *gambaru* found in specific situations is related to the discourse about emotions. By being told or by saying that one has 'persisted' or 'persevered', the emotions of satisfaction at personal accomplishment coupled with the feeling of support from others is differentiated and given the name of *gambaru*. In other words, saying things about persistence is a mode of linking the positive emotions associated with such situations to the schema of such actions. Later on the children associate and remember elements of *gambaru* through these lived experiences which have been 'talked through'. To reiterate a point I made in the previous chapter, there is (to be sure) a biological basis for the feelings and emotions involved, but it is the link to certain socially defined goals and models which is of importance here.

Finally, I would argue that the *gambaru* 'complex' gains motivational force by being related to the other key schema which is being internalized by the children (and which has its own motivational force) 'groupism'. Take the following example:

> During school sports days (*undookai*) vigorous competition between classes of children and even between the mothers or fathers of a class is enthusiastically encouraged by the teachers, principals and spectators watching the races. In these events the feeling of group solidarity experienced by the losers, who commiserate with each other *Zannendakedo gambarimashita* ['It's too bad, but we did our best'] is perhaps even more keenly felt than is the collective sense of group accomplishments of the victors (Tobin *et al.* 1989: 41).

Here the point is not only that *gambaru* serves the goal of creating a group, but that some of the satisfaction at having persisted has to do with satisfaction and recognition at having 'grouped'.

The Life-course Perspective

An emphasis on the schema of perseverance is found throughout

Japanese society: in stories pertaining to the formal school curriculum (Lanham 1986; Gerbert 1993); in preparations for entrance exams to high schools and universities (not in their content but in the intense experience of exam preparation that is believed to strengthen an individual's character and moral fiber); in wide public and governmental support for school-based moral education (Singleton 1989: 11); in exhortations of government officials to citizens during sports days (Ben-Ari 1991: 215); in programs of spiritual education in companies (Rohlen 1986); in special ethics retreats catering to people who have adjustment problems in their current lives (Kondo 1990); and in the context of old age homes as expressed in the personal power to survive through forbearance (Bethel 1992: 123). Kondo (1992: 45–6) sums up the 'adult' notion involved in *gambaru* through the expectations of traditional artisanship: becoming a mature practitioner of the trade, she tells us,

> means having to undergo hardship (*kuroo*) for only in this way will the inner self be tempered . . . *Kuroo* can be found in carrying out the requirements of a social role, whether it be the role of bride, mother, or worker [or preschool pupil]. The hardship of a young person in training for the university entrance exams can be a form of *kuroo*. So can the tribulations of a young bride who leaves her natal family to become a member of a new household.

It is this aspect of the inculcation of *gambaru* that is related to the long-term strategy of teachers in preparing the children for school and for life. According to them, the ability to persevere is a prerequisite for functioning later on in life, for it is at those points where *gambaru* appears later on that people draw upon what they have internalized during childhood experiences.

Moreover, as we saw, these experiences also involve internalizing a motivationally relevant discourse, a set of terms with which to make sense of reality. To take up a point suggested by Rohlen (1986), programs of spiritual education for new workplace recruits (and by extension, the ethics retreat that Kondo describes) reinforce, exaggerate and use what the participants have already experienced. In these and other adult situations, *gambaru* becomes – like the ability to group – a strong source of satisfactions and frustrations and a source of self and other evaluation. It is this schema which is used later on in life by people in workplaces, by brides entering an extended family, or by citizens in sports days to evaluate their own and others' performances. I found a good example of this point in the words of the deputy head of Katsura Day-Care Center. She told me of the intense difficulties she had encountered when she had moved into a new *hoikuen* in the past. The only way she had survived, she noted, was by "persevering" and overcoming the initial difficulties.

Conclusion

Gambaru, like the schema of grouping, is inculcated in a variety of contexts that both reinforce each other and give the schema its richness. Like acquiring the ability to group, so learning to persevere involves internalizing a set of body practices and linking these practices to a set of motivating experiences. It is in this light that the connection between *gambaru* and both boring situations (like dressing) and more interesting activities (like play) should be seen. Let me be clear that I am not arguing that in other preschool systems the children do not learn how to wait, how to overcome their desires or how to function in groups. What happens in Japan is that these abilities are learnt through an intentional set of practices and explicitly related to a motivationally relevant discourse about perseverance and groupism.

This point concerns my perspective on the body and embodiment. Persistence, it should be stressed, includes both a dispositional aspect focused on the constraints of the body and a volitional one centering on action. To take off from Turner (1992: 95), the children learn to handle both the 'body as constraint' and 'the body as capacity'. In this sense my analysis extends beyond Bourdieu's (see Turner 1992: 91) whose emphasis on habitus is deterministic: a system of dispositions with reference to a given place which produce regularities in modes of behavior (the body as a bearer of cultural codes). As I showed, in understanding *gambaru* there is a need to account for action and intention because persistence involves innovation and application to new situations. *Gambaru* thus involves learning how to act autonomously within the given constraints of the body. I develop this theme in the next chapter.

Notes

1 On one occasion one of the teachers of the three year-old children made two youngsters sit in this position for a full 45 seconds so as to quieten them down before continuing with a class song.

2 The emphasis on *gambaru* is moreover, evident in such mundane activities as eating with chopsticks, cutting with scissors, preparing one's bag for returning home or folding a towel after swimming. As Peak (1991a; also Tobin *et al.* 1989: 193) notes, the pedagogical purpose of teaching children how to dress themselves is primarily one of cultivating the ability and willingness to persevere.

The Marathon

The following event took place during my first period of fieldwork in Japan. On a cold Wednesday morning in February 1982 we were invited to our son's day-care center to support and participate in what was dubbed a "marathon". My wife and I arrived at forty minutes past nine together with a man who was the grandfather of two girls from the center. Along with some other parents we waited in the rather spacious grounds of this suburban *hoikuen*. Dressed down to their underwear and jumping and stretching, the children from the age of two and upwards were all clustered in one of the rooms and warming-up for the run. When the exercises were over, the head of the *hoikuen* gave a brief talk to the children: she praised their participation in the marathon, asked them to be careful while running, and to try as best as they could to finish the run.

Spaced out in intervals of 30 seconds, groups of children went outside, put on their shoes and lined up at the start of the route: a street next to the center. At the start of the circuit stood two teachers and about 60 or 70 meters away stood two other teachers whom the children were supposed to touch before running back to the starting point. As the children were being prepared, the assistant head teacher handed the parents flags made by the children (painted in colorful hues) and asked us to disperse along the route and wave our flags. Parents kept arriving during this stage as well, and all in all about twenty-four adults participated (apart from the teachers).

The children received an explanation about the route, the need to run to the teachers at the midway point, to touch them (but 'in a way that doesn't hurt') and to run back. Each age-group began its run together with the class teachers. The parents quickly dispersed along the way, waved their flags, and shouted '*ganbatte*', or '*faitto*'. Thus as the children were running they were supported and encouraged by the teachers, parents and later by the children who had already completed the course. Everyone ran, including the smallest children who often held teachers' hands. There was little competition between the children and the aim was to run a full ten minutes for the older children and a little less for the younger ones. Some of the parents and a few teachers took pictures.

Then the parents were asked to take their coats off and to run as well. Joking a little to offset our slight embarrassment, we ran only one time to and back from the midway point. This was an opportunity for the children to wave flags and to cheer us on. Once this part was over, the children went into their respective home-rooms and took their clothes off and, to the accompaniment of a song on the cassette player, massaged themselves with a towel over their heads, necks, stomachs and feet. Then to the accompaniment of another song they massaged each other's backs. The song ended and everyone got dressed.

The parents were invited inside to the center's hall for the closing ceremony in which the children received a certificate of participation in the marathon. Each child was called to the front and given a certificate stating his or her name and the successful completion of the run. Each and every child was applauded as they went to the stage. The head teacher thanked everyone for their participation and made a special note about the perseverance ('*yoku gambatta*') of the children. Then, group by group the children were photographed. The children were asked to say '*chiizu*' (cheese) so that their mothers would be happy with the pictures. As the children returned to their normal schedule the parents returned to work or home.

Chapter 6

Eating to Become Japanese
Body, Habits and Organization

Introduction

This chapter is an analysis of mealtimes – primarily lunch and afternoon snacks – at Katsura Day-Care Center. I have chosen this focus in order to recapitulate and to exemplify the theoretical proposals that have been developed in earlier chapters. Empirically speaking, I show how these earlier propositions may further our understanding not only of sleep or play, but of other domains managed by preschools. But what kind of theoretical questions can be addressed through focusing on food and mealtimes? Three sets of issues suggest themselves in this regard: the relation between food and *childhood*; the *institutional* context of this relation; and its specifically *cultural* character.

It has now become a rather commonplace social scientific notion that the production, preparation and consumption of food carry a variety of moral, social and aesthetic meanings (Douglas 1984: 5; Symons 1994). Here, however, I will not summarize the major avenues of research that studies of 'culinary culture' – the ensemble of attitudes and tastes people bring to cooking and eating (Mennell *et al.* 1992: 20) – have pursued. Rather, I suggest that one consistent emphasis found in this scholarly literature bears upon my analysis. As Murcott (1984: 2) observes, social scientific studies have consistently illuminated how during certain critical periods of the life course (infancy, childhood, pregnancy, and old age) food is closely related to matters like etiquette and deportment, health and nourishment, and social relations and ties. Indeed, Valsiner

(1987: 157 emphasis removed) proposes that childhood is especially important in this respect because "mealtimes are one of the very few recurrent settings in the lives of developing children where they experience the cultural organization of the social life of their culture in its full complexity". These observations suggest the first set of questions which guide my analysis: how are assumptions about the proper development of children related to eating practices? How are these notions reproduced through preparations for and the organization of mealtimes?

Such questions, however, do not progress much beyond those addressed by many model studies which have centered on food in the family and in the home (for example, Newson and Newson 1974; Charles and Kerr 1988). A no less important problem is one of understanding mealtimes in *institutions* of early childhood education. Food practices in these institutions are intriguing because of their 'interstitial' character:

> On the one hand, they are settings which stand in contrast to the public commercialized world of eating out. On the other hand, they stand in contrast to the home-cooking in the household domain of the personal private and intimate. At the same time, institutions are to stand for the domestic sphere, at least in some measure (Mennell *et al.* 1992: 112).

As I showed in Chapter 3, the 'interstitial' nature of pre- schools lies in the developmental role they are seen to carry out: they are charged with managing the movement of children from the family into the 'wider' world. It is at this point that the second set of questions which direct my analysis emerges: how is the 'in-betweenness' of preschools related to the conventions governing meals and mealtimes? How are these conventions related to the practical accomplishment of organizational goals?

Yet the complexity does not end here, for my focus is on a *Japanese* preschool. During the past decade or so a number of scholars have dealt with specific aspects of food in Japanese preschools. Joy Hendry (1986a) for example, mentions mealtimes as part of her overview of childhood socialization. Peak (1991a) shows how eating is related to the general set of Japanese practices designed to discipline children and to get them to adjust to the routines of preschool. Fujita and Sano (1988) analyze the organization of meals in order to understand the cultural assumptions about childhood development which mark the Japanese context.

These studies – containing a host of insights but no comprehensive examination of food in Japanese preschools – provide the background for the third set of questions guiding my analysis: what are the *Japanese* cultural assumptions about food that are inculcated in preschools? How is the organizational context used to propagate and inculcate these notions?

My thesis. The preparation and consumption of food is used as a major means for the socialization of youngsters around the world. Hildebrand's (1986: 450–65) much used textbook is but one American example of the view that educational goals can be achieved through children's experience with food. However, what I argue in this context is that some of these goals vary cross-culturally to fit distinctive notions of proper eating behavior and that these goals are implemented in ways that are consonant with the overall aims of preschools. More specifically, I contend first, that in Japanese preschools food is explicitly and implicitly related to goals of inculcating a sense of group belongingness, absorbing notions of responsibility, and learning the organization and aesthetics of 'typical' meals. Second, that imparting eating habits involves harnessing the basic physiological processes of the children so that they gradually master self-control and self-reliance. Third, that mealtimes are a major avenue through which an orientation to the peer group (and more generally, the outside world) is added to the orientation to the family. And fourth, that teachers mobilize and control mothers in and around food related issues in order to assure the proper implementation of all of these educational goals.

Mealtimes at Katsura Day-care Center

There seems to be a marked similarity in the typical meals provided in preschools throughout Japan, and Katsura *Hoikuen* is no exception (Peak 1991a: 90ff; Fujita and Sano 1988: 81–2; Hendry 1986a: 136). Food enters the institutional lives of children primarily during lunches and (less elaborate) snacktimes. Barring the occasional picnic or outing, lunches invariably take the same form. Each age group congregates in its classroom after the plates and large utensils (supplied at Katsura by the center) are distributed by the teachers and the daily rotating monitors (*otooban*). The children then carefully place the chopsticks, cups and cloth napkins which they bring from home on the table in front of them. The children are supposed to wait quietly during this period of preparation, and once everything is ready they sit down and sing one or two songs. The monitors are then invited to stand up and lead the class in a short prayer and in the fixed phrases announcing the beginning of the meal (*itadakimasu*).

The food is served by the teachers and (according to the ability of the age group or of a particular individual) by the monitors. Thus for example, while the children of the five year-old group pour tea for their friends, the youngsters in the three year-old group are allowed to hand out things like rolls or little cookies. Each item is usually served in a separate plate or bowl. Mealtimes are lively with the children often talking about such things as television shows, family trips, and new games. In this way the youngsters learn to enjoy the relaxed circumstances of companionship in meals in which they share personal experiences with others of their group. While teachers often participate in these conversations, they are also very aware – as was made apparent to me during staff meetings when the eating habits of children were discussed – that they are acting as role models for the children. As one teacher told me, "meals (*shokuji*) are also education (*kyooiku*) and culture (*bunka*)". If there is enough food, children may ask for second helpings, but must line up properly and ask for the additional portion in a polite manner.

Lunch typically includes potato salad and fish, chicken or beef and vegetables, noodles with meat sauce or small pieces of pork, *miso* soup and *toofu*, *tempura* and rice, hamburger and salad, or fried noodles (*yakisoba*). Afternoon snacks include (salty) rice crackers, small (Western) cookies, bean cookies, or fruit (like bananas or tangerines). The preferred method of preparation is simmering and as a consequence the food is unlike much of the greasy institutional food our son was served in English preschools. Rice is served on most days but bread or pastry are occasionally provided for variety. In fact, children often close lunch with rice which is consumed either with pickles or with *furikake* (shredded seaweed, fish and seasonings).

The end of the meal is again marked by ritual expressions of appreciation (*goschisoosama deshita*) which like the premeal phrases seem to be used to a greater extent throughout Japan than are terms of grace in Britain (Hendry 1986a: 77). Cleaning up is carried out by everyone under the orchestration of monitors and teachers: the plates collected and returned to the kitchen, the garbage sorted into recyclable and nonrecyclable items, and the chopsticks, napkins and cups are placed in the children's bags to be taken home. Finally the children proceed to wash their faces and brush their teeth.

'Civilization', Aesthetics and (Cognitive) Order

At their most obvious, eating practices involve a set of processes which may be termed – to borrow from Norbert Elias (Elias 1978; Mennell *et al.* 1992: 3) – a 'civilizing process'. While Elias focused on the manner by which the body was historically rationalized – through table manners, norms of good conduct, and etiquette – I suggest that in Japanese preschools (like such institutions around the world) eating practices are one of the central methods for turning children into 'civilized social beings'. As Peak (1991a; 91) notes, meals are seen by government officials as an integral part of the preschool curriculum and as constituting a valuable lesson in basic daily habits and the customs of group life. Indeed, according to government guidelines – the Ministry of Health and Welfare for day-care centers and the Ministry of Education for kindergartens – acquiring proper eating habits is one educational goal of pre-schools. But what are the aims of this 'civilizing process'? And what are the actual processes by which the children are turned into civilized beings?

A central aspect of socialization related to food is teaching the children about the cultural organization and aesthetics of typical meals. In this respect the center reinforces and further develops the notions that the children have been taught at home. Take four ideas which lie at base of the cognitive order of such meals. The first notion is related to the centrality of rice (or more rarely noodles or bread) as the 'definer' of a meal (Ashkenazi 1990: 441). This situation stands in contrast to (mainly) Western societies in which it is the meat or fish dish which forms the basis of a meal.[1] Accordingly, children in Japanese preschools learn that in order to be categorized as a 'true' meal, rice must be the key ingredient (and thus that snacks are just small food events in between main meals).

A second, and closely related notion focuses on the proper development of children. When discussing the menu that was constructed for the infants, one of the cooks asked me if I had ever heard the term *rinyooshoku*:

It means to wean them [the infants], to separate them from milk and to introduce food which is different from milk. During this period we have to prepare special things for the babies. At the beginning it is a soup, an *omoyu* [a water thin rice gruel] that is an extract from rice. Then we thicken the rice little by little so that at the end they can finally begin to start eating rice. The next stage is a kind of gruel (*okayu*) and then a soft rice (*nanpaku*). In this manner we gradually increase the amount of rice we give the children. In the end we give them regular rice, and by the time they enter the group of one year-old children they can eat rice.

Here rice is seen as a designator, by means of consumption via the body, of Japaneseness (actually all East Asian cultures). To make the reasoning of this passage clear: while the developmental axis of weaning is found cross-culturally, to become 'truly' Japanese is to be weaned *towards* rice.

The third notion has to do with Japanese ideas about the proper presentation of food. In the case of typical Japanese meals a different dish – the actual physical container – is used for each portion or serving. Indeed, this kind of notion is echoed in the organization of *obentoo* (lunch) boxes which are usually divided into different compartments for each portion. I was given an interesting illustration of this point when the three year-old children were served bread. The monitors were directed to place each piece of bread on a tiny tray and to hand out these containers to the children. In this way, bread was integrated into the cultural logic of mealtimes through being placed in a separate dish.

The fourth and final point is that given the organization of typical meals, children go on to learn the proper way of manipulating the separate dishes so that they create the sequential order of the lunch. Japanese meals partake of a sort of simultaneity in the sequence by which the food is eaten, and offer a contrast to the (Western) concept of precedence as in the appetizer-main course-sweet rule (Ashkenazi 1990: 341). In Japan, all the portions are served concurrently (in separate dishes) and the children learn to eat the portions together: for instance, meat, rice or pickles interspersed with spoonfuls of soup or cooked vegetables. But the children do not only learn the composition and presentation of proper meals, they also absorb the import of food as a social signifier.

Groupism, Commensality and Responsibility

Food, as a host of scholars have noted, stands at the core of sociality (or its lack): who, when and how one sits with to eat carry certain messages. Just as the more formal dining lists of educational establishments reveal certain notions of institutional commensality, hierarchy, and participation (Goody 1977: 132), so arrangements at Katsura *Hoikuen* betray ideas about group identity and membership. Seating order is the clearest indicator of these notions. Not only do the children sit together in class groups everyday, but even on special occasions (picnics and outings) although there are few explicit directives to do so, the children tend to congregate in the same groupings. In this way both the inclusiveness and exclusiveness of the class circle is emphasized. Moreover, as part of the stress on impartiality within the group, teachers are careful to allocate their and visitors' seating 'attendance' evenly between the different tables. For example, whenever a student trainee or myself joined a class we were allotted our seats according to a general notion of previous apportionment.

Katsura *Hoikuen* offers a contrast to the American day-care center studied by Tobin and his associates (1989: 134) where, as part of an emphasis on getting children to express their individual wants, youngsters were offered a selection of dishes. At the center (like other Japanese preschools) children are offered no choice of edibles: each meal is a 'set menu' of drinks and portions which the children consume. In this respect, Peak's (1991a: 93) observations about Japanese preschools hold for Katsura *Hoikuen* as well: a great deal of care is taken to ensure that each person eats identical food so that 'mutuality and common preferences are affirmed'. A related notion underlies the considerable pressure which is exerted on children to participate in the formalities marking the beginnings and ends of meals. In fact, toward the end of my fieldwork I witnessed a full five-minute tussle between a teacher and a child who refused, and eventually capitulated, to saying the beginning grace with the rest of the class.

Another fascinating manifestation of the group emphasis is the treatment accorded to *omiyage*, souvenirs brought from one's travels. At Katsura *Hoikuen* teachers invariably, and the children sometimes, brought back souvenirs from trips to places as far away as Hokkaido or as nearby as Osaka. The *omiyage* brought back were almost always foodstuffs such as sweets, crackers or cookies.

While the custom of *omiyage* is found throughout Japanese society, the manner in which these edibles were allocated at the center is instructive: the sweets were not eaten according to individuals' discretion but invariably consumed in group contexts at the end of lunch or snacks. Moreover, each teacher or child brought souvenirs for her or his class and not for members of other classes. In this manner food is used as a medium of exchange – through the long-term effects of mutual gift-giving and gift-receiving – to reinforce the stress on group identity.

All of these explicit and implicit practices form part of the consistent stress of Japanese preschools on creating a strong identity between the child and the class as a whole, on inculcating a sense of group life (*shuudan seikatsu*). But as I showed in Chapter 4, in creating group life the transmission of messages about common identity is not enough. As Rohlen (1989a: 26) observes, of equal importance are routines designed to foster sentiments of cooperation and collective responsibility. As noted earlier, a number of commentators have recognized the central role of rotating monitors (*otooban*) in furthering the educational goals of Japanese preschools (for instance, Fujita and Sano 1988: 85). These monitors carry out such tasks as leading class greetings, helping to record attendance, and organizing the children for various activities. Katsura *Hoikuen* provides an example of how the *otooban* carry out assignments related to food and mealtimes and how these duties are related to the general aims of such institutions.

On a 'technical' level, monitors are responsible for such things as reporting the number of attending children and teachers to the kitchen, fetching and handing out portions, pouring drinks, leading the class in songs and formalities, and helping to clean up. While these tasks differ according to individual children's abilities, teachers are insistent that the youngsters make an effort to carry out as many of the assigned duties as possible. To give one example, when one *otooban* was too shy to lead the class in the premeal grace the teacher did not allow the other children to help her; and the child eventually mumbled the words along with the teacher. Most of the children, however, very readily carry out the role of monitor, and as in the day-care center studied by Fujita and Sano (1988: 82) take great pride in fulfilling this role. Mealtime assignments are thus part of a wider range of *otooban* tasks by which preschools motivate children to specific actions by inculcating a sense of personal responsibility for group duties.[2] Moreover, the fact that *everyone* undertakes this role reinforces the group emphasis of the preschool.

Responsibility is inculcated in many other ways. Cleaning is done by children and their class teachers and not by specialized staff (not even the cooks who rarely venture out of the kitchen). Like similar routines in Japanese elementary schools (Cummings 1980), the fact that caretakers and pupils do the actual cleaning contributes to a recognition of the importance of such work and of the obligation to carry out tasks allocated to the class as a whole.[3] At Katsura *Hoikuen* this emphasis is strengthened by making sure that individuals take responsibility for their own actions: whenever youngsters spill something teachers insist on them cleaning up. In one instance when a five year-old girl did not want to clean up the milk she had inadvertently spilled, the teacher took her hand in hers and together they knelt to clean up the milk.

Another means for imparting a sense of responsibility is the cultivation of a tiny vegetable garden in the yard. The group of oldest children (I was told that everyone would be included if the center had a larger yard) are divided into four circles that grow tomatoes, eggplants, pumpkins and cucumbers.[4] Once these vegetables have grown they are taken to the kitchen and served to all of the members of the center. A related practice is one of occasionally pairing 'healthy' and 'disabled' children. The former are expected to aid the latter in such matters as setting the table, sitting properly or cleaning up. In this way the resources of the children in and around mealtimes are used to integrate disadvantaged children into the class.

Seen within a long-term perspective, however, the routines and practices related to mealtimes are related to the interstitial character of the preschool. Like the sleeping habits examined in Chapter 3, so mealtime habits and conventions form part of the processes by which children are conveyed from the relatively protected home to the external world. Tobin (1992: 26) quotes the traditional saying: "To become a (mature) person one must eat a stranger's rice." For the children, mealtimes during the first phases of attending preschool imply sharing and eating with, and being served and serving, strangers. It is only gradually that this group of strangers becomes the group of significant peers. By eating with others, the children gradually learn not only the differentiation between cognitive categories of intimacy (*ura*) and formality (*omote*) or ingroup and out-of-group (*uchi* and *soto*). Along the lines suggested in earlier chapters, they also learn to embody the movement between these categories and to be motivated to do so.

Self-Mastery and Social Control

While all of these things are going on, another set of processes operate towards achieving a subtle combination of self-control and self-reliance which are the substance of a disciplined (Japanese) child. Bryan Turner (1992: 4) suggests that one cannot understand the disciplined mind without understanding the disciplined body. Along the lines outlined in the previous chapter, I contend that mealtimes predicate a gradual harnessing of the children's bodies – their limbs, capacities for coordination, and cravings, for instance – towards actions and demeanor considered socially 'proper'. This point seems to bear special import in the context of Japanese preschools because, as Peak (1991a: 91, 94) observes, much of the stress on self-reliance and self-control outside of the home is seen as a corrective to the informal and mother-dependent eating habits to which most children are accustomed.

Around the ages of two or three rather specific kinds of self-control and self-reliance are introduced. Take the kind of self-control required of the children when they wait for the tables to be prepared, the food to be apportioned, and the group to sit down quietly. The children are usually very hungry and thirsty, and overcoming their cravings is often a difficult task. In fact, while waiting the children are often told to persevere, to be patient (*gaman*). Similarly, after the meal, teachers will not allow the children to wash their cups and chopsticks and brush their teeth if they do not wait properly (that is, in a quiet and orderly manner) for their peers. The point of these exercises is not to reinforce the external authority of the teacher (although this element is also involved) but to help the children internalize self-regulation.

Next, take the complex progression from finger feeding to the use of utensils such as chopsticks. From the age of about two and a half children begin using chopsticks. During the initial stages of use, chopsticks are wielded in one of two ways: either as an implement similar to a fork in that pieces of food are pierced and brought to the mouth; or as a shovel for pushing food from the serving dish brought up to the mouth. In both cases even these 'inappropriate' methods are still difficult for the children because they must discriminate the right amount of food that is manageable for one intake. In fact, these methods are seen by the teachers as a stage between 'eating like a dog' (bringing the head close to plates on the table) and eating properly with chopsticks.[5]

Later, as the children grow older, their food is served after being cut up into bite-sized pieces so that there is no need for knives and the pieces can be picked up with chopsticks. But even in such cases it often happens that a piece of food is larger than would fit into one bite and the children are taught that they can pick up the whole piece with their chopsticks and hold on to it while eating with the food next to their face. Consequently, it is in the use of utensils that the cultural organization of eating becomes most intimately intertwined with the children's developing motor behavior (Valsiner 1987: 174). The children not only learn to control their bodies, but by learning to use chopsticks (as an extension of the body) do this in a manner that is seen by teachers and parents to be quintessential Japanese.

The etiquette of eating also forms a central focus for combining self-regulation and cultural conventions. In all of the centers that I visited, I found children receiving large doses of instruction on table manners. Youngsters are taught the politeness forms required at the beginning and at the end of meals, the terms used to address persons serving food or the proper sitting posture. Moreover, teachers use the children's desire for second helpings to reinforce these messages. To give one example, when one three year-old boy wanted a second helping of some rice balls he was made to stand straight without fidgeting, to ask the monitor in a proper manner. (*kudasai* and not *choodai*), and to thank her when he had received his additional portion. In a like manner, teachers often use the children's liking of sweets (jelly, ice-cream, or crackers, for example) as a means to cajole them to proper manners. Quite often these desserts are withheld until the children behave according to the teachers' expectations. One child, who wanted ice-cream had to finish the pumpkin that was on the day's menu before receiving his helping of the dessert.

As these last examples show, self-mastery is achieved through the active and intentional use of techniques of control by teachers. Teachers do not only serve as role models for the children but 'positively' exhort and encourage them. More 'negatively' they set clear definitions of, and limits on, unacceptable behavior. In my fieldnotes I have recorded many instances of teachers directly commanding the children to do or to stop doing a variety of things: 'don't talk loudly', 'sit down', 'stop talking', 'start eating', or 'finish up'. The words of one class teacher were typical in this respect. During lunch she addressed a three year-old boy: "Don't prick and play with the tomato! Don't pick it up with your fingers, but use your chopsticks." In another case a boy from the group of four year-old youngsters, spilled some rice on the floor. The class teacher asked him "Why do you play like that? It's not good to play that way. Why did you throw it down?" She then brought some paper tissues and together they cleaned up the rice. She used a combination of direct and indirect methods of discipline: while directly addressing the boy's misdemeanor she then helped him to clean up by putting her hand on his and going through the motions of tidying up together.

If this point sounds obvious, I think it should nevertheless be stressed against the background of – mainly American – portrayals of Japanese preschools. Perhaps stemming from their attempt to come to terms with the questions of how such institutions differ from American ones, such scholars as Lewis (1989; 1991), Tobin (1992) and Peak (1989; 1991b) have tended to stress the 'soft' or 'motivating' methods of discipline in Japanese preschools. As a consequence, they have tended to underplay the ubiquity and importance of 'hard' or 'direct' methods by which children are controlled. It appears that the disciplinary methods used in regard to eating seem to involve more 'negative' sanctions and direct commands than those used in the direction and supervision of play and games: in a word, eating episodes are characterized by greater surveillance and regulation. The reasons for this situation, I would suggest, lie in the notion that during such occasions the biological and animal side of the children may surface (nature) and thus have to be most clearly domesticated (culture).

A complementary method of public control and guidance involves the peer group (see Peak 1991a; 132). Peers gather class members for meals, hurry children who are late, or silence noisy neighbors. Class fellows consequently serve to reinforce the children's sense that pressure for appropriate behavior comes not only from significant others like teachers but also from their peers. In one preschool she visited, Hendry (1986a: 136) observed that no child begins eating before the premeal "ritual has been enacted, and children who misbehave are reprimanded by their friends . . . The more time it takes to complete the preparations, the hungrier they get, so it is to the advantage of all that things run smoothly, which makes for very effective peer group discipline." I found a fascinating example of the role of monitors and peers in another Kyoto day-care center that I visited. The head teacher told me of a boy who did not want to eat. The solution they hit upon was to occasionally turn him into the monitor of one of the groups of younger children. These younger fellows thus served as agents that subtly pressured him into 'taking responsibility for eating properly' and he began to eat more regularly.

Controlling Mothers

So far my focus has been on interrelationships between children and teachers. But there are other actors that are involved in the organization of meals and in the inculcation of proper eating habits. Fujita (1989) has raised the question of how mothers are controlled and socialized through preschool education. Here I take her question and apply it to a number of issues as they bear upon eating and food.

Let me begin with the use of eating utensils and eating posture. While taking rather subtle form, teachers often use commentary about children's mastery of chopsticks to discuss the responsibility of mothers. A number of times (and at a number of preschools) I heard teachers complain that mothers tend to entrust the task of teaching the children how to use chopsticks to the teachers. One caretaker went so far as to relate this to the laziness of mothers and to their lack of commitment to fulfilling their parental role. The deputy head of the center (a woman in her forties) explained that "today, many young mothers do not teach their children even basic things like not putting their elbows on the table when eating". "And", she continued, "they themselves eat in this way." During an interview with a young teacher (this was her second year at the center) I asked about the parents' role in children's upbringing:

> Well everything, upbringing in the wide sense of the word: they teach the children how to eat, how to do everyday things. We [teachers] help them to bring up the children.

Along these lines, conversations during pick-up times at the end of the day repeatedly centered on issues of food. Teachers often advised mothers about the best ways to improve their children's eating habits and in this way gained mothers' compliance with their perspective. In a similar vein, the occasional criticisms I heard about mothers' practices of serving their children slapdash TV dinners were related to how they were not fulfilling their motherly role. Interestingly then, as in other industrial societies, worries about the decline of the family are often talked about in terms of the decline of the family meal (Mennell *et al*. 1992: 116).

﹀*Obentoo*, packed lunches, also figure in the control of mothers by preschools, although this point may be more important in kindergartens where mothers prepare lunches a few times a week than in day-care centers where children arrive with such boxes only once or twice a month. Peak (1991a: 59) reports that at a kindergarten she studied (mothers there prepare *obentoo* four times a week) the governing expectation was that such meals be attractively prepared, nutritionally balanced and fit the developmental stage of the children (for instance, the rice balls must be of a size that can be easily picked up).

But there is more here. As Peak (1991a: 60) notes, "the preparation of *obentoo* becomes both a primary symbol of the loving concern appropriate to the mother-child relationship. And it is an important means of socializing Japanese mothers in participating in their child's school activities and demonstrating concern for their psychological well-being while away from home". Indeed, the head of Katsura *Hoikuen* once explained to me that while the reason for bringing *obentoo* only once or twice a month was that mothers are busy working, they (the mothers) "nevertheless always put up a good show. The children often show me the lunches they have brought from home". Indeed, the children, very proud of their mothers' creations would often display them to me and to their peers. Mothers, in turn, knowing that the *obentoo* they have prepared will be open to public scrutiny, are thus exposed to what Tobin, Wu and Davidson (1989: 66) term the political pressures to conform.

The day-care center our son attended is a case in point. There, children were supposed to bring cooked rice from home while the rest of the daily meal was supplied by the preschool. At the beginning of fieldwork, my wife and I simply sent him with white rice in a small lunch box. After a few weeks, however, the teachers took my wife aside one day and patiently explained the need to decorate the white rice so that it will seem appealing to our son. My wife was even shown an example of a model lunch box (prepared by another mother) in which the white rice was capped by two slivers of red pepper with a green olive at their intersection. Moreover, the teachers advised her that we could add things like *umebooshi* (salted plums) when sending the rice with our son. Through following the teachers' advice we learnt both the aesthetics of preparing *obentoo* and the proper side dishes that go with rice.

Conclusion

As in other cultures, so in Japan it is widely assumed that 'habits', 'behavior' and 'preferences' related to food which are acquired in childhood shape those of adulthood (Mennell *et al.* 1992: 58). In the Japanese context, this general assumption is joined with more specific notions about what it means to become Japanese, to give form to a set of practices found in and around preschool meals. Accompanying an assumption about food answering the need for physical sustenance are ideas about proper etiquette, pre- and post-meal formalities, the use of utensils such as chopsticks and dishes, mealtime organization, and the centrality of rice.

But, as I argue, the 'civilizing process' of children does not only involve grasping these sets of symbols and categories. It also involves harnessing certain physiological needs and desires, and physical capabilities and potentials towards the inculcation of body deportment and movements that are considered 'proper'. In all of these cases, the teachers use a combination of positive incentives and negative sanctions in order to motivate the children to eat properly.

The institutional dimension of food preparation and consumption is related to issues of commensality as a basis of group identity and responsibility. In addition, in the Japanese context, because preschools offer a *contrast* to the home and to what is expected of children at home, the role of preschool is of prime importance in guiding the movement of children from the family to the wider world. It is for this reason that preschool teachers control and guide mothers (and more generally family life).

Notes

1 Properly speaking then, while it makes cultural sense for a Japanese person to ask me whether I eat rice, or bread or potatoes in Israel, this kind of question is improper according to my native manner of categorizing meals.

2 Such is the sense of pride and responsibility associated with this role, that our son who attended a small government run center at the beginning of the 1980s wanted to attend his day-care center on the day he was slated to be an *otooban* even when he was sick.

3 Moreover, through straightening up by themselves the children learn appropriate cultural notions of cleanliness and the different types of cloths used for floors (*zookin*) and for tables (*fukin*).

4 At the center our son attended in the early 1980s the garden was cultivated jointly by the children and members of the neighborhood's old-folks club (Ben-Ari 1991).

5 In a related vein, children are gradually taught to pour liquids so that by the end of the process they can handle whole cartons of milk.

Interlude IV

Menus

What are the order and contents of meals in preschools over large spans of time? How is the monthly or yearly schedule of menus prepared? The basic food needs of children are defined in Japan, as in all industrial societies (Charles and Kerr 1988: 108), as biologically determined and natural phenomena. For example, just as men 'need' different kinds and quantities of food than women, so there are types and amounts of edibles which are appropriate to children. I was given numerous examples of these notions in interviews with Katsura Day-Care Center's two cooks. In these interviews, both women conceptualized the process of constructing menus in terms of how proper nourishment contributes to sound development. Thus for instance, when I inquired about serving fish, they replied that the reasons are their high calcium content – contributing to healthy bones – and and their plasticity – strengthening the children's jaw muscles when chewing. More than vague assertions about health and well-being, these comments are grounded in a well developed body of knowledge called nutritional science.

Japan is no exception among the industrialized countries in witnessing the growth of nutritional science after World War II. Partly related to the development of the welfare state, "nutritional science comprises aspects of biology, microbiology, biochemistry and biophysiology. Its outlook is very practical, setting itself health goals in the first place; as such it can be seen as a specialized part of medical science" (Mennell *et al.* 1992: 36). From our perspective, what is of import is that experts in nutrition link food to health by setting 'good' standards for edibles. These standards are deemed to be especially important during crucial periods of the life course such as childhood. Bryan Turner (1992: 178) suggests that the link between the expertise and knowledge of this science and the micro level of food intake and eating habits may be understood through the diet as a regimen: that is, a regulated diet that reflects both the government of food and the government of the body.

In all government run or government controlled day-care centers in Japan, cooks must obtain a license (over and above the regular caretaker's license) from the prefectural government before they are allowed to begin working. Licensing involves passing a test based on government run seminars or workshops and specially prepared textbooks and reading material which are based on the recognized body of nutritional knowledge. Once working, such women continue to use this knowledge as it appears in a host of cookbooks, tables, charts, and suggested menus. In this way, cooks become the practitioners of nutritional science. Cooks at preschools like Katsura *Hoikuen*, to make this point clear, are thus not 'experts' but operative agents whose expertise involves the practical use of nutritional science in institutional contexts.

At Katsura, moreover, some of the food is provided by a *kyooshoku senta* – literally center for the provision of school lunches. The center, which supplies food to other day-care centers and some small factories in the area, transports its edibles to Katsura daily in a small van. While the *hoikuen* prepares things like fried rice, soups and vegetables, the meat and bread are usually provided by the *kyooshoku senta* which also furnishes detailed recipes for various dishes and detailed charts of the caloric and nutritional content of different dishes. An additional constraint is financial: cooks at Katsura *hoikuen* like all such institutions, write a 'school lunch diary' – open for occasional inspection by the head of the day-care center or by government officials – where they record the purchase of all foodstuffs. Menus can thus be used (as part of wider inspections by external government officials) to monitor the manner by which the regulated diet of children is constructed.

These circumstances are related to a wider trend of stand-ardization of food in contemporary Japan. In contrast to older regional variety, a national version of institutional food reflects the homogenization of meals through the regulations of government ministries, the reports of the national media, and the procedures of food preparation centers. More concretely, because institutional cooks consult, and are constrained by, such nationally available written material to extend the range of dishes they prepare, children in various parts of the country eat more or less the same kind of food. Because recipes have become depersonalized and have acquired a more universal nature, food has become rather standardized. In addition, the trend towards industrial food has reduced differences within and between socio-cultural systems (Goody 1982: 189). Thus, just as a great deal of preparation and cooking of food is now carried out in specialized factories and plants before it reaches the home, so much of the work that was previously done in preschools is now done in specialized institutions like the *kyooshoku senta*.

I was given a fascinating example of the 'delocalization' of food (Mennell et. al. 1992: 76) as an outgrowth of international food industries through the case of Milo – the chocolate drink. Milo, like all industrially produced food products is manufactured in order to make a profit. When I carried out fieldwork, the company making Milo was making an effort to promote their product in Kyoto's preschools. I saw a poster advertizing the drink in Katsura *hoikuen*'s entrance room. The deputy head explained that the teachers' had decided to try the drink and that from its powder they would be able to prepare such things as puddings, jelly, cookies (*warabi mochi*) and chocolate drinks. This product was something new in Japan, she added. The incorporation of such products as Milo should not be understood simplistically as some kind of uniform process. The adaption of Milo for local cookies or the accommodation of curry rice to local tastes are but two examples of the Japanization of international food (see also Ashkenazi 1990). What does seem to have been happening in the past decades is the national homogenization of food.

Against this background we may understand how the monthly menu – a presenter or meals to come (Goody 1977: 133) – is constructed. While of regular and often repetitive shape, the variation of the menu over the long run is made to fit the developmental trajectory of the children. In an interview, one of the cooks explained how each month's schedule is prepared:

We check the caloric content, the fat and the proteins of the food. We are allowed a certain amount of money per day for each child by the government which is different for children below and above the age of three; this allocation is based on 22 days of providing lunch and afternoon snacks. We set the menu

more or less according to the average intake of basic items that
the children are supposed to obtain everyday: a minimum of
meat, sugar, fish, bananas, fruit . . . Again these are different for
children below and above the age of three.

She then showed me the many tables and charts describing the
vitamins and nutritional content of different edibles. Finally, she
displayed the special menus that they construct for handicapped
children and the lists of youngsters with allergies to such things as
milk, eggs, or soybeans.

Once the menu is in existence, it can be used to achieve certain
correctional ends. For instance, the menu, or more correctly the
notions embodied in it, are used by the teachers to identify a
variety of physical and familial problems arising in an economically
affluent consumer society. For example, two of the problems
teachers related to the intake of junk food were obesity and
maldeveloped teeth. Along the lines I outlined in the previous
chapter, these difficulties were often related to mothers' responsibility in giving the children such food.

Food is related to yet another level of public discourse in
contemporary Japan. Two interrelated sources of health problems
identified by the teachers are the Westernization and industrialization of food. Take the words of one the cooks:

> There are all sorts of problems with calcium intake recently. This
> trend is part of the Westernization (*yooshiki*) of the eating habits
> of Japanese children, so that we get all sorts of problems like
> cavities and rotting teeth. We wouldn't have these problems if
> the children ate traditional things like beans or *toofu*.

She continued on to what she perceived as the problematic nature
of 'industrial food' in institutions of early childhood education:

> Some parents want us to prepare everything here at the day-care
> center by ourselves. They don't want us to receive anything from
> the food preparation center. They want us to serve more natural
> food (*shizen shokuhin*) . . . You know, recently, we find many
> more allergies because of all of the stuff they put in food these
> days. Children have become allergic to such things as ice-cream
> or mayonnaise.

Indeed, at the center which our son attended this matter was
constantly raised in meetings and in pleas to the head teacher. On

one level, such statements should be understood as part of the greater 'health consciousness' which marks contemporary Japan. Since the 1970s a host of Japanese health food movements – like similar programs the world over – have embodied suspicion of the industrialization and chemicalization of foods (Mennell et. al. 1992: 25; Ben-Ari 1991: 39–40).

Interestingly, however, on another level other issues are subtly introduced into the debate about the value of manufactured food. In such statements as I have just quoted above, mothers and caretakers tend to conflate small-scale preparation with a lack of chemicals. They tend to conflate the materials with which edibles are prepared and the social context of preparation. As Charles and Kerr (1988: 130) observe in regard to home-cooking, the "way food is categorized depends not so much on the end product . . . but on the process of production that a certain food has undergone, and who has performed work on it". Expending time and effort on the production of a meal in the home thus in some way confers goodness on it: "perhaps a moral rather than nutritional goodness" (Charles and Kerr 1988: 131). Applied to my case, the governing assumption at the base of parents and teachers' plea for food prepared at the day-care center seems to be that such food is closer to home-cooking and *therefore* better. Perhaps it is the 'interstitial' nature of institutional cooking in preschools – between the commercialized world and the home – which makes it a prime arena for debates about the virtues and vices of different kind of food preparation. The head of the day-care center, well aware of this situation, noted

> The food from the [school lunch] center is not in itself bad. We eat a combination of food from that center and what we prepare here, but there is no guarantee that if we prepare the food here it will be good. You can also prepare natural food from the portions sent from the lunch center.

But if, as Goody (1982: 2) says, food involves "placing oneself" in relation to others, then the naturalness which is desired by teachers, cooks and parents is also a way of placing themselves in relation to Japan's past. Thus another theme which was occasionally raised by caretakers and parents was a nostalgic desire for a return to the natural and healthy food of an imagined past. As in the cook's statement about the virtues of the traditional diet of beans and *toofu*, so the food of Japan's yesteryear appears to be

both scientifically and nutritionally sound and culturally
appropriate.

Atkinson's (1984: 12) point is that the imagery of natural food "is
not simply a way of 'packaging' health foods or making them more
attractive: rather, it is constitutive of their supposed efficacy in the
promotion of health and the remedy of disorders". The category of
nature is not culturally uncontaminated, but draws

> on a wealth of images of rural and urban living, in which the
> contrast is made to do service to convey moral messages: the
> contrast between rural order and urban chaos, between natural
> virtue and degeneracy. The very imagery of the adulturation of
> 'pure' food with synthetic additives is preganant with such
> associations (Atkinson 1984: 15).

Thus in contemporary Japan, discussions about the virtues of
'traditional' food should be seen as part of a much wider public
debate about the goodness of the past and the ills of industrialism
(see Ivy 1989; Martinez 1990; Robertson 1992).

Chapter 7

Name-Calling
Power, Play and Classification

Introduction

In this chapter I lead the discussion of bodies and the body in a
different direction. I examine the interrelationships between three
elements of Japanese culture: power, play and classification. More
specifically, I focus on the behaviors of what Schwartzman (1978:
25) calls the 'child as critic' or what Kishima (1991: 82; Fratto 1976)
would call 'tricksters' in Japanese preschools. Such behaviors
include the variety of witticisms, obscenities, jokes, satirical jests,
name-calling and general mischief that form an essential part of any
child's life. I undertake an analysis of such playful behavior for two
reasons: first, because such conduct has hitherto received relatively
little attention in the study of Japanese preschool education; and
second, because an analysis of such actions raises critical questions
about our very conceptualization of (Japanese) children and just
what it is that goes on in such institutions.

An examination of how children play with power and classification seems to be especially important in regard to academic
studies of early childhood education in Japan. These studies have
tended to portray Japanese preschools as social mechanisms that
prepare youngsters for an assortment of future roles such as school
pupils or company employees. Thus even when scholars note the
relatively chaotic nature of Japanese kindergartens and day-care
centers they do so in terms of how such disorder contributes to the
children's development. Sano (1989: 127–8), for example, suggests
that underlying the apparent chaos of day-care centers is good

classroom management which utilizes both the resources of teachers and the children to make day-care goals more effective.
Tobin (1992: 30) notes that periods of apparent disorder and silly
and uninhibited play are coupled with periods of order so that the
children learn to distinguish contexts and the behaviors appropriate
to them. Indeed, in an essay with Wu and Davidson (Tobin *et al.*
1991: 30), the term 'developmentally appropriate chaos' is used to
characterize the period of preschool as mediating the sheltered life
of home an the tumult of the real world. But what of 'developmentally inappropriate behavior' such as irony, jokes, satire, and
subversion? How do they fit the order and disorder of Japanese
preschools?

In the best of current (mainly American) anthropological
tradition, let me begin with myself. I do this not in order to regress
into an amateur form of self-analysis, but because I think that the
way I was 'handled' in the field may teach us something about the
themes of power, play and classification.

(My) Names

I must confess that I have always had trouble with my name. Some
forty years ago my parents immigrated to Israel and after I was
born, a year or so later, decided to give me a modern Hebrew
name. Eyal means something like 'strength' or 'power', while
Ben-Ari means 'son of lion'. This is certainly a fitting name for a
child growing up in a new country bent on creating traditions and
protecting its existence. But it is not such a convenient name for
someone who travels the world and who comes into contact with
people speaking languages other than Hebrew.

The trouble began in English-speaking countries with my
personal (sometimes erroneously called Christian) name. I have
been called such things as Iyal, Yael (a woman's name), Ayal
(which means ram), and all the way to El-Al which is the name of
our national airline. In Japan for some reason, the troubles seemed
to focus on my family name, and I have often been called Ben-Ali
which, to my Israeli ears, sounds like an Arabic name: son of Ali.
Thus when I went to do fieldwork in 1988 a Japanese friend kindly
suggested that to make things simpler I introduce myself as Ben Ari.
Hence at Katsura *Hoikuen* I became known as Ben Ari sensei, Ben
sensei, or Ari sensei. Again to my ears this abbreviation of my name
sounded a little funny, like 'Ri' which could stand for Hendry or for

Raveri, but I agreed because I thought it would make things easier. I was mistaken. This point was only the beginning of a set of transformations that my name underwent at the day-care center.

The beginnings of these transformations involved my physical size which, to put it understatedly, is at least a cut or two above that of the average Japanese nursery school teacher (I am 190 centimeters tall and weigh over 90 kilograms of brain, muscle and fat). A week or two after I arrived, one little three year-old boy stood next to me. He looked up, held his index finger to this thumb, and with a twinkle in his eye said something along the following line:

> *Ari* are ants, and ants are very small animals; so how can such a large teacher (*ooki sensei*) be a teacher of such little ants. How can you be a teacher of ants (*Ari no sensei*)?

Later, as the children became more familiar with me, they began to play with the 'Ben' in my name. I did not mind being called *benkyoo no sensei* (a teacher of study) and I did not really mind being called *obentoo no sensei* (a teacher of lunch boxes). But of course, the most obvious connection (which I did not foresee at the time) was to the toilet and to excreta, for I was soon dubbed *benjo no sensei*: a teacher of the toilet. As though this was not enough, every once in a while I was called *unchi no sensei* or *unko no sensei* (a teacher of poo-poo or poo-pee) or even *oshikko no sensei* (a teacher of wee-wee or pee-pee).

But then a further development ensued. Every once in a while, I would be standing next to one of the teachers when a child (or more rarely a group of children) would run past us and in a stage whisper utter one of my 'names': *benjo no sensei* or *unko no sensei*. The teacher standing next to me would often smile in somewhat embarrassed silence, and the youngsters happy at this effect, would run off. As I then noted in my field diary, I sensed that during these episodes, the presence of the teacher was of importance.

I found these micro-episodes of name-calling fascinating, and began to ask myself questions about their wider implications. But these were not questions about myself. I am not too macho and it did not really bother me to called these names. Rather I felt that this name calling could teach me something about the organization and social order of the day-care center.

Playful Transformations

The first thing that I did when I began to write this chapter, was to look at my fieldnotes for other examples of such behavior. This review is important in order to both to understand the ubiquity of such behaviors, and to understand the situations within which they emerged. At first I found what may seem to adults to be 'funny' or 'cute' episodes: a boy turning a set of chairs into a train on the Hankyu line and proclaiming '*Umeda tomarimasen*' ('This train does not stop at Umeda station'); or a little girl in the pool taking a cup of water and in all seriousness mimicking the television commercial with '*otoko wa biiru*' ('Men are [for] beer'). While both instances involve the transformation of concrete materials (chairs into trains and water into beer) I felt that my name-calling was akin to a different type of behavior which went on all day at the center.

Out of the tens of examples I have recorded in my fieldnotes let me briefly outline the following few. The first type involved playing with the center's resources in direct contravention of teachers' directives and definitions. Thus, during lunchtime chopsticks were changed into planes; during snacktime biscuits were turned into cars; on a picnic rice-balls were turned into bombs; and during a Montessori session (the center was toying with the possibility of turning into a Montessori preschool) wood pieces were converted into missiles.

The second type had to do with a slight alteration of normal activities. One afternoon the group of four-years old children were preparing to leave the day-care center at the end of the day. The teacher sat down at the small organ, and we began to sing a rather well known song called 'Sayonara' (goodbye). About halfway through the song a group of 3–4 youngsters began to sing off key and to overstress the words. As they received a rather appreciative reaction from their peers, they continued to 'ham it up' for a good few minutes. The teacher had to repeatedly ask them to desist before they finished the song in the proper way. Similarly, in another group, as roll call was taken, the children shouted their responses – '*hai*' – in ever exaggerated tones with one child trying to outdo the other. On another occasion a six-years old girl was sweeping the floor when she encountered a teacher and myself who were standing in her way. Sweeping our feet, she reacted: "Oh, the amount of large garbage (*oogata gomi*) you find in this place!"

A third type of behavior revolved around toying with the educational goals of teachers. Before entering the pool, a particularly strict teacher (one perhaps more prone to literal mindedness) was showering the children with cold water. As the water hit him, one of the prime 'jesters' from the five-years old group began to shout '*atsui, atsui*' (hot, hot). The teacher, believing it her duty to inculcate the proper use of vocabulary among her charges, patiently explained that the proper term was '*tsumetai*' (cool), but the more she explained the stronger he shouted '*atsui*'. In this way not only did he succeed in exasperating her, but also in eliciting gales of giggles from his classmates. Similarly a teacher asked "we will do something nice today, do you know what it is?" meaning entering the pool. One little trickster answered her in a logical if nonsensical manner, to the laughter of his friends, "yes sure, juice. Juice is a nice thing!".

The last type of playful behavior resembles my name-calling most closely. This behavior entails playing with the 'self' of the teachers and openly flustering them. Along with name-calling such behaviors included pulling at teachers clothes or untying the knots at the back of their aprons; following teachers to the bathroom and shouting '*oshikko, oshikko*'; pointing out their physical attributes like big butts or small breasts; or sitting behind them and saying 'I saw your butt' ('*oshiri mihata*' in the local dialect).

What I want to get across by providing these examples is an idea of the ubiquity of a certain type of play behavior in the life of the *hoikuen* I studied (and by extension of any such establishment). As is evident from these short passages, such actions are imaginative although not in the sense of the formal curricular activities designed to foster creativity: painting, music, dance, or storytelling, for example. Rather, these creative performances and acts seem to emerge alongside other activities. They tend to be considered bothersome or at the very least unimportant within the situations in which they emerge. To follow Kishima (1991: 110), the creativity of these actions seem to lie in the deformation of context.

In order to understand these behaviors and their implications I think it important to begin with their 'mechanics', their 'internal logic'. In my analysis I will use the example of the name-calling I was subjected to. I emphasize, however, that I am using this *one example* as an entry point for a wider exploration of all the types of action I have outlined.

The Logic of Humorous Criticism

At its most basic, I think that name-calling is a form of humorous criticism, of joking. Joking is defined as the conscious or unconscious transition from one meaning structure to another, without changing much of the original meaning structure (Zijderveld 1968: 290). To put this point by way of my case, the children linked the meaning structure related to the teacher or educator to the meaning structure of the bathroom. They did this through the very common Japanese form of punning or play upon words called *goroawase* (Backhouse 1976: 149). In *goroawase* a sequence of sounds is associated with a similar sequence of sounds of different meaning. In educational establishments, *goroawase* is often used as a device for the memorization of numbers. In my case it was used to achieve a different goal: to put into question the authority of the teacher.

How was this done? Teachers in Japan have a special status which is grounded in two qualities: (1) the general Japanese sensitivity to, and stress on, social positioning and status appellations in hierarchical order (Lebra 1976: ch. 5; Smith 1983: 74ff); and (2) the relatively strong sense of respect and honor still granted to teachers in contemporary Japan. Indeed, parents and children use the term '*sensei*' when calling teachers rather than using their personal or family names, and head teachers are often called *encho sensei*, i.e. by their organizational role. Through using these formal designations, parents and teachers reinforce the notion of the importance of their social position as teachers.

Along these lines, by putting the rather 'exalted' figure of the teacher in the bathroom, one begins (like the children in Katsura *Hoikuen*) to see things in a different light. As the English term captures it, teachers come to be seen as 'base': that is, not only without dignity or sentiment but perhaps also basically human and therefore as equal to children. In calling me a teacher of the toilet then, the children inverted the usual hierarchy of the preschool.[1] In addition, of course, they also (unintentionally) used the mnemonic device of *goroawase*, which is commonly employed in achieving formal educational ends, to suit their own purposes. In this way name calling – not always sophisticated, not always conscious – is predicated on playing with classification. But notice that what the children achieved was not a total negation of the formal role of teachers. Rather name calling – like all irony and satire – involves a 'double vision' (Babcock 1984: 108). It is not merely a matter of seeing some 'true' meaning beneath a 'false' one but of seeing them simultaneously. Teachers are, at one and the same time, both hierarchically positioned and essentially 'like' the children.

But given that name calling often embarrasses the teachers – that is, puts them in a situation where they are somehow impeded in carrying out their role – it also appears to involve power. And an examination of power leads us from the 'mechanics' of joking to the place of critical play in the wider social order of the center.

Play in Official Categorization

The way I would like to approach this issue is to ask about the manner by which critical play is labelled and categorized by teachers. My assumption is that, to a large extent, official definitions form the basis for *actions* caretakers undertake in reaction to mischief and to humorous criticism. Where does one discover such official definitions? I propose that they may be found in one of the least researched areas in Japanese organizational life in general and Japanese educational establishments in particular. I refer to the numerous, almost bewildering, array of records, forms, files, and memos found in such institutions (Ben-Ari forthcoming).

It is difficult to get across the importance and pervasiveness of these texts. The following is but a short list of the documents which the highly literate teachers fill in, or read, every week:

Yearly, monthly, weekly and daily outlines of curricula.
Timetables for teachers' duties.
Administrative reports on the center as a whole, for each group, and for individuals.
Intake questionnaires for children entering the center.
Reports on children going to school the following year.
Letters and notices sent home and back.
Records of roll call.
Medical certificates and reports.

From our point of view the most important texts are the following:

Checklists for appraising development.
Checklists for identifying problem children.
Individual charts which include data on such matters as eating and sleeping habits or social interactions with peers.

What is the role of these texts? I suggest that they are a primary means through which the developmental theory of the day-care center is put into effect (Ben-Ari 1995). Forms aid teachers in classifying the ongoing behaviors, processes and interactions of the *hoikuen* into discrete categories. Such documents enable teachers to name and label children as belonging to one or another category according to prevailing professional (and wider social) standards. But these documents are not only mechanisms for classifying the world. Because these texts contain practical formulas they are also the means that help teachers to handle children – that is, to treat them in what are taken to be developmentally appropriate ways (Handelman 1981). In this manner, teachers classify children and children's behavior on the basis of a theory of 'natural' or 'normal' growth as embodied in forms and documents and then, on the basis of comparing these children and their behaviors to the theoretical 'norm', decide to take suitable action.

But what is the theory of natural or normal child development that is embodied in these forms?[2] For a variety of historical reasons modern lives have come to be defined – by the state and its representatives – as a *course*, as a linear movement (Mayer and Muller 1986). As the term human *development* implies, lives are conceptualized in this theory as comprising movement along a series of rather precisely circumscribed events, states, qualities, and capacities. At their beginning various theories of human develop-ment – be they of the sociological or psychological varieties – were essentially descriptive and analytical. But through a variety of mechanisms – the work of experts and advisors, therapists and applied social scientists, and the media and popularizers – these theories have been turned into normative constructs. Once accepted into the prevailing culture, they no longer operated simply as descriptions of human nature and its growth. They have become accepted cultural criteria by which social reality is ex-plicated, made sense of, and evaluated (Bruner 1986: 134).

What I am saying is that when rendered into organizational arrangements, child development theories turn from a theoretical 'is' to a practical (and very powerful) 'ought'. Documents based on current theories of child development enable teachers to label, define, and name those children who are 'running' late or 'running ahead' (Roth 1963). For instance, if a checklist tells you that by the age of one or three years of age a child should be doing this or that, a teacher or caretaker can take the appropriate measures to deal with the 'deviance' of the child from the purported norm. To put these points by way of the case of Katsura *Hoikuen*, over time, the collection of daily charts filled in for each individual form a text that documents a child's behaviors, allows them to be systematically compared to those of other children, and facilitates teachers' proper handling of these behaviors.[3]

Harkness and Super (1983: 5) suggest that cultures differ in their choice of the goals seen as critical for growth and the developmental issues which are seen as the most important for each stage. Applied to our case, we may ask what is the place of humor, jokes, criticism, and satire in the teachers' professional theory – as embodied in the center's documents – of 'normal' development? Accounts of play as they appear in the center's documents, are overwhelmingly accounts of what from the official viewpoint, may be termed 'developmentally relevant behaviors'. In other words, to be defined and categorized as *significant*, play has to aid the 'normal' growth of children. Specifically, three developmental goals were seen as relevant to play: motor skills, as for example in the increasingly complex use of fingers in arts and crafts; general abilities, like the power to concentrate for longer periods and to complete puzzles of growing intricacy; and the ability to 'group' as in the case of newcomers who gradually come to participate in class activities. In all such accounts, to take up Mechling's (1986: 97) suggestions, play and games are seen as training grounds for adult life in bureaucratic industrial society.

But what of play behavior that does not fit this kind of categorization? In a few cases, such demeanor is defined as behavioral incompetence or as an impediment to normal development. Remember the child who shouted 'hot, hot', when showered with cold water. The assistant head of the *hoikuen* later told me that he is a bit 'slow' (*okurette-iru*). His mischievous behavior was categorized as inappropriate to the normal trajectory of growth. Indeed, in a number of charts and personal documents, this child was classified as a slow learner and as having speech difficulties. Without belaboring the point, it is sufficient to note that most of his subsequent behavior came to be interpreted in terms of this initial labelling.

On the whole, however, playful criticism was either ignored or labelled as 'mischief' or 'nonsense' (*itazura*). Thus at the same time, as no mention whatsoever of critical behavior appears in any documents at the center, teachers (if they verbalized anything at all) mentioned its basic nonseriousness.[4] It seems that the underlying assumption is that such things as satire and irony, or jests and jokes are developmentally irrelevant. This assumption finds corroboration in the general notions of 'obscene' jokes. In a study comparing preschools in Japan, the United States and China we find:

> We should perhaps mention . . . that penis and butt jokes were immensely popular with four year-old children in nearly every school we visited in all three countries. The only noticeable difference was that such humor was most openly exhibited in Japan, where the teachers generally said nothing and sometimes even smiled (Tobin *et al.* 1988: 88).

Here we have a situation in which critical play and banter are pervasive in institutions like Katsura day-care center, yet are almost totally ignored in official viewpoints. If this is so, then what are the implications of how teachers 'unsee' (or less extremely, disregard) such behaviors for the *academic* study of early childhood socialization?

Play, Politics and Academic Analysis

By beginning from an assumption that engaging in developmentally appropriate behaviors is necessary in order to learn to function in society, many studies conceptualize children as being somehow incomplete. As MacKay (1974; also Toren 1993: 471) notes, youngsters are variously immature, irrational, incompetent, asocial, or acultural all depending upon whether you are a teacher, sociologist, anthropologist, or psychologist. According to this view children are seen as 'needing' to be brought up, to be completed according to adult notions of what it means to be complete. The consequence of this situation is that there is little research which seriously takes into account the role of children as active and independent agents who participate in (their *and* in adults') socialization.

One aspect of the independent activity of children is their disruption of, and challenge to, the taken for granted world of adults. Their knowledge often contradicts what adults claim is 'obvious' 'known' or 'accepted' to 'everybody'. For this reason children are a constant political problem (Waksler 1986: 74). If we understand the political problematics of care-taking we begin to appreciate that socialization may be a far less certain process than is commonly imagined: it is an interactive process with participants at times engaged in a struggle rather than in a one-sided relation of helping, leading, or nurturing (Waksler 1986: 75–6). These points are particularly important in regard to many studies of early childhood education in contemporary Japan.

Take for example the special issue of the *Journal of Japanese Studies* [Winter 1989 15(1)] edited by Thomas Rohlen and Catherine Lewis and entitled 'Social Control and Early Socialization'. These (consistently superb) articles were the first contributions about socialization to appear in this journal (with its own pretensions to represent the best of Japanese studies in the world). Note the titles of the papers:

Rohlen: 'Order in Japanese Society: Attachment, Authority, and Routine.'
Boocock: 'Controlled Diversity: An Overview of the Preschool System.'
Fujita: '"It's All Mother's Fault": Childcare and the Socialization of Working Mothers in Japan.'
Peak: 'Learning to Become Part of the Group: The Japanese Child's Transition to Preschool Life.'
Sano: 'Methods of Social Control and Socialization in Japanese Day-Care Centers.'
Lewis: 'From Indulgence to Internalization: Social Control in Early School Years.'

This collection is enlightening in two respects. First, it underscores American society's interest in – some would say, pre-occupation with – social control. Without embarking upon a full-blown critique of mainstream culture in the United States, let me provide another indicator of the stress on control. The following excerpt is from Fujita and Sano's (1988: 88) cross-cultural study of caretakers in American and Japanese day-care centers:

The strongest impression of the Maple [the American center studied] teachers have is that the Japanese center is too noisy and looks even chaotic . . . The Maple teachers think the reason for these disorderly behaviors must be due to the high child/teacher ratio. With that high ratio, the Maple teachers feel that there is no way the teachers can adequately control the children. One reason for their concern about control is to maintain a safe environment for children.

The second point I want to make about the studies appearing in

the *Journal of Japanese Studies* (which are representative of much
of the scholarly work being currently carried out) is more general.
The underlying view posited by such titles as 'Learning to Become
Part of the Group', 'Methods of Social Control and Socialization', or
'From Indulgence to Internalization' is one formulated in terms of
what the children ought to be (and ought to become) rather than
what they are. Thus what is of prime interest is not the independent
organization, critical capacity, or resistance to imposed normality of
children, but rather their conformity and obedience to, or their
voluntary consent to a variety of educational measures aimed at
turning them into fully functioning Japanese adults. The central
focus in such studies is, to borrow from medicine, the 'ortho-
paedics' of early childhood education: that is, the correction or cure
of deformities and diseases of childhood in the name of educational achievement (Brinkman 1986).

American early childhood education – and this point is made
most explicitly in the essays by Lewis (1989) and Rohlen (1989b) –
is seen as being able to benefit from Japanese methods. Thus for
instance, Rohlen (1989a: 2) points out that the roots of impressive
cognitive achievements in Japan are to be found in the preschools
and first grades of primary schools where 'order' is established.
Partly a consequence of a nostalgia for the way things used to be
in the (Western) past, and partly an outcome of a real willingness
to learn, the subtext of many studies of Japanese institutions of
education is 'how and what we can learn from Japan'. Catherine
Lewis is the scholar who has been most explicit in stressing this
view in regard to Japanese preschools. In another essay on the
transition from home to preschool, she states that one of her major
aims is 'to stimulate American thinking' about aspects of education
in Japan (Lewis 1991: 81). In her review of Lois Peak's excellent
book, Lewis (1993: 154) again asserts that a major (but not the only)
question that the book raises centers on the implications of
Japanese practices for American preschool education. (I leave aside
her assumption about excluding non-Americans from this debate.)

It may now be clearer how critical play, name-calling, and
naughtiness may be defined within this perspective as problems to
be dealt with by using a variety of methods of social control
(including positive techniques based on teachers' patience). It may
also be clearer how within this viewpoint children are seen as
objects to be dealt with, or as political problems, rather than as

autonomous persons who are partners in socialization. This point is pertinent to more general models of Japanese society. The recent work by Bachnik and Quinn (1994) is a case in point. In various parts of their volume these scholars make an excellent case for conceptualizing Japanese culture in terms of ongoing processes of negotiation. Thus for instance, rather than positing a fixed set of meanings at base of this culture, Bachnik (1994) suggests that concepts of inside and outside, front and back, or formality and informality are actualized in specific situations by actors. What is missing from her analysis however, is an appreciation of the manner in which people – adults and children – may question the very basis of such concepts. In other words, her model fails to account for how jokes, irony, or parody may challenge the very basis of what she terms the 'distance cline'.

At this point a word of caution should be sounded. I am not arguing for an unqualified rejection of what has been written about childhood and education in Japan. I simply assert that by adding my perspective, we may gain a much richer appreciation of what, to borrow from Joy Hendry (1986a), it means 'to become Japanese'. Along these lines, I return from the rather abstract critique to the case of name-calling.

Play at the Center

Let me begin with the assumption that through playful criticism children gain a measure of control over their own lives and participate (as active agents) in their socialization. If this is our starting point, then the negotiations over power implied by such conduct would seem to involve the following layers of analysis.

Play in itself

On one level, it is apparent that the children often enjoy mischief for its own sake. This kind of play is close to Huizinga's notion of play not being goal oriented but an aim in itself, or what Mulkay (1988) calls 'pure humor': a continual and pleasurable activity in which, when prolonged, participants often become increasingly animated. This enjoyment may be of special importance in word play (Kirschenblatt-Gimblett and Sherzer 1976: 7), in which the center of interest is a process rather than a goal. The process is not designed to achieve educational ends – as are most of the activities based on the formal curriculum – but is voluntarily elaborated and complicated in various patterned ways. Hence, for the children, the transformation of my name from a 'teacher of ants' to 'Mr. Pee-pee' (through a variety of permutations) had entertainment value because it allowed them both to express their inventiveness and to discover (along the way) that the transformations could be extended continuously.

In such cases, from an adult point of view, the children carve out for themselves a 'senseless' enclave of autonomy for the sheer enjoyment and the unproductive entertainment of the activity. Moreover, *because* the activity is labelled by adults as 'senseless' the children are free to carry it out without much interference and it is perceived (by adults) as not threatening the everyday, serious order of the center.

Play against order

But this is only one level, for at the same time name-calling and related actions take place *against* the rational and goal-oriented activities of the center, and *against* the teachers and their professional agenda. Hamming up a song, or turning rice-balls into bombs, to formulate this point by example, are done in opposition to stipulated rules and definitions. Another example is the 'misbehavior' during roll call that I described earlier. Tobin and his associates (1989: 189) recount the normal, taken-for-granted norms of linguistic behavior in Japan:

> Language in Japan, both in an out of preschools, is divided into formal and informal systems of discourse. Children in preschools are allowed to speak freely, loudly, even vulgarly to each other during much of the day. But this unrestrained use of language alternates with periods of polite, formal, teacher directed group recitation of expressions of greeting, thanks, blessing and farewell (Tobin *et al.* 1989: 189).

Against this background, it is understandable that the children choose to use precisely these junctures of relatively high formality for their diversions: funny faces, or answering teachers in exaggerated tones. It is expressly because such situations as morning assembly are taken by the teachers to be serious that any distraction is all the more effective.

In a related vein, embarrassing and questioning the authority of the teachers form part of the playful interaction *with* the teachers. Take for instance, adults' embarrassment which is induced by children's prodding. The important element here is the link between the children's action and the teachers' reactions. In such cases adults are manipulated by youngsters in the same way that the latter would operate a toy. But teachers are better than toys in that their responses are unpredictable, and in that they are in a position of authority. I was given a good example of this point when one caretaker played cards with a few members of the three year-old group. The object of the game was to match pairs of cards, and it began well enough. But after a few minutes, the game degenerated into a free-flowing contest with no real rules and no real goals. The youngsters seemed to be enjoying the teacher's efforts at getting them to take the game seriously. After a few more minutes the teacher left and the game ceased to be interesting for the authority figure was gone.

Play and the peer group

The next level of analysis has to do with the group context within which play takes place. Indeed, in most cases it is as important for the peer group to be present as it is for the teacher to be attending. There appear to be three elements at work here. The first is, as Corsaro (1988: 3) points out, that peers share their control through play. In this sense added to the entertainment created by teachers' reactions is the fun of eliciting responses from peers. From the peers' point of view, there is the added possibility of vicarious participation in the performance of a 'bad' deed by a friend. One afternoon, a three year-old boy picked up the bell used for summoning the children for morning roll call and, with his face full of mirth, began to ring it. He not only played with the organizational arrangements of the center, but entered into an impromptu session in which a number of other children joined in to caricature the behavior of the assistant head teacher's behavior during morning assembly.

The second element is related to how play acts to create a community spirit among the children at the expense of another group, the teachers (Fine 1988: 52). In this sense, children actively generate the groups they belong to (politically speaking, they constantly create coalitions), but through means not explicitly intended by their teachers. The peer group is important in a third sense because it provides the social means for a young individual to achieve status. Aggressive pranks are thus not only acts directed against people who control children, they are also related to the internal social dynamics of the peer group. To follow Fine (1988: 47), in critical play, the goal is not always to do harm but may also be a way for a child to gain renown for being daring.

Shock value

This leads us to the fourth level of play. Let me get at this point through obscenity. One does not need, as Mechling (1986: 98) says, a Freudian perspective to recognize that the child's body is a powerful symbolic territory. Children endure early pressures towards socialization to oral satisfaction and control over bowels and bladder. Obscenity thus has great expressive benefits for children for the 'shock value' it affords because it is basically subversive. It subverts many of the educational emphases on the mastery of the body and of body comportment that I have been examining throughout the book.

But the subversive quality of obscenity does not only lie in its 'shock value'. Obscenity, like all critical play, is subversive because it can emerge anywhere and anytime. More generally, all such behaviors are threatening to the everyday order because of their unpredictability. Because jokes and jest, and mischief and prankishness are by their nature 'free-flowing' they can emerge in any situation including the most serious and consequential ones. Critical play then is always a political problem because of its potential for mobile (in all senses of the word) resistance.

The limits of subversion

For all of this, however, one should not overstress the subversive aspect of play. To do so would mean losing sight of the extent and the mechanisms by which children in preschools are controlled. Children may question, they may criticize, but ultimately they are unable to change the practices which concretely affect their lives. Their criticisms are politically impotent (Fine 1988: 51) for a variety of reasons such as their lack of organization, lack of commitment and uniformity, small physical size, tight controls adults have over them and the rewards constantly offered to those who conform. Like the acts of caprice carried out by workers described by Kondo

(1990: 213), the children's mischief are little episodes of resistance through which the power of those in authority is both undermined and consolidated.

Conclusion

The criticisms, irony, obscenity, and name-calling that I have outlined here may violate certain popular and academic notions of Japanese children. Their sheer ubiquity and dynamism however, underscore how central they are to the ways in which youngsters relate to their lives. To paraphrase Helen Schwartzman (1978: 12), teachers and educators (and most of the 'experts' they depend on) tend to view such play behavior in terms of what it is not: not work, not real, not serious, not productive and not contributive. My contention is that much of our social scientific understanding of socialization in general, and in Japan in particular has adopted this view of critical play.[5]

In contrast to this prevalent view, my argument is that acts of caprice and questioning should be seen as constitutive of pre-schools to the same degree as their formal organizational hierarchy, division of labor, and curriculum. In this respect, the official view of critical play is part of a rather ironical situation. It is precisely because such behaviors as satire, irony and obscenity are not seen (by caretakers) as 'real' and as 'serious' that they can be used to explore themes not open to children in the everyday, common-sense, taken-for-granted world of preschool. In other words, children are rather free to criticize such things as teachers' pretensions to authority and order because their critiques are taken to be non-serious.[6]

If we adopt this vantage point, we begin to perceive Japanese preschools in a slightly different manner. We realize that, like the lives of Kondo's (1990) workers, so the lives of Japanese children are rife with contradictions and ironies: they constantly conform and criticize, obey and disobey. The range of behaviors examined here all contain a potential for children to assume a critical stance towards the day-care center. In these creative incidents the ironic twists of meaning and the challenges and ambiguities of life emerge for these children. In this manner we begin to appreciate the variety and the complexity of the experience of early childhood education in Japan.

Notes

1 Kishima (1991: 84ff) gives a similar example of a government minister who was caught by a press photographer urinating against the wall of the Diet building. He was soon dubbed *oshikko daijin* (lit. minister pee-pee) and the term helped him appear to be an unpredictable and loveable fellow among other stark, sombre and pretentious politicians.
2 Here I follow Bruner (1986: 135) who suggests that theories of human development "may with profit be examined in the same spirit in which an anthropologist studies, say, theories of ethnobotany or ethnomedicine".
3 To be sure, I am not arguing against the utility of many such forms as diagnostic tools that help turn children's lives into fuller, and richer ones. As Hobbs (1975: 5) notes, classification and labelling are essential to human communication and problem solving. I do not suggest that all abuse or rigidity in classifying will disappear when such texts disappear, I simply argue that if we uncover the theoretical assumptions that lie at the base of such documents we may better understand the ways organizations such as day-care centers work.
4 Peak (1991a: 141) relates an incident in which a teacher explained to her that the mass table pounding that had just taken place was just "simple, 'primitive' fun".
5 Indeed, these assumptions underscore the idea that both the preschool and the workplace are essentially similar sites where serious and productive work is undertaken.
6 In fact, the same kinds of critiques are voiced by workers toward their bosses and organizations during drinking parties. Because such parties are defined as nonserious, employees are comparatively free to voice their complaints (Ben-Ari 1993).

An Instance of Discipline?

An incidence from my fieldnotes summarizes several of the socialization strategies discussed above. A number of boys were fashioning clay 'bombs' and dropping them on the class's goldfish. The teacher explained to the boys a number of times that they could hurt the fish but did not specifically tell the boys to stop (nor did they). The teacher discussed the incident with the whole class at the end of the school day, explaining that some boys thought they were helping the class by throwing in clay that looked like food, but that the boys were actually harming the fish. The teacher suggested that the whole class make sure the fish were cared for well. When I subsequently interviewed the teacher, our exchange was as follows:

> Int: Did you really think the children were trying to help the fish by throwing in clay pellets?
> Teacher: Yes.
> Int: Don't you think the boys understood they might hurt the fish by throwing the clay pellets?
> Teacher: If they understood it was wrong, they wouldn't do it.

The teacher's failure to require, or even request obedience, her involvement with the whole class in discussion and management of the incident and her unwillingness to attribute bad motives to the boys illustrate the socialization strategies discussed above. (Lewis 1989: 148)

Chapter 8

Conclusion

In this volume, I have dealt with a set of central issues related to socialization in Japanese preschools. I have carried out my examination through a case study, that of Katsura *Hoikuen*. In the introduction I located my analysis within a broad move that has marked the social sciences in the last few years: a shift to studying the body and emotions. My aim, however, has not been to add yet another polemic note to this debate but rather to utilize the empirical world of early childhood education in Japan in order to do two things: to formulate a set of theoretical insights into these themes; and to apply these insights to further our understanding of socialization in such institutions. After very briefly recapitulating my theoretical stance, I draw out three wider (and perhaps more speculative) themes which are interwoven throughout the volume.

First, I examine the organizational context within which habits and emotion are inculcated. Understanding this context is important because it brings in the dimensions of power and discipline involved in socialization. At the same time however, we must be careful of seeing these processes only as the outcome of conscious and intentional manipulation on the part of teachers. Next, I suggest a way of thinking about the long-term effects of preschools through linking the concept of cultural scenarios to body practices and to emotions. Such a conceptualization may aid us in discussing these long lasting effects without assuming a deterministic relation between childhood and adulthood. Finally, I relate the issues of play and resistance to notions of Japanese selves. Here I propose that looking at preschools through a political model aids us in uncovering the space for personal autonomy and individual independence that is expressed by Japanese people throughout their lives.

Embodiment, Motivation and Internalization

Theoretically, my project answers recent scholarly calls for a recognition of the centrality of the body in social processes (Blacking 1977; Turner 1992; Csordas 1993): the need to theorize and conceptualize the manner by which different body practices and emotions are constructed in social settings. Thus the challenge, as I explained in previous chapters, is not just to invoke the label of 'embodiment' but to carefully place the issues involved within a theoretical framework and then apply this framework to further our understanding of socialization.

The first (and crucial) issue is the importance of the inner experiences of children in socialization because it is through these experiences that the link between cognition, emotion and motivation is best understood. Within the disciplines dealing with cross-cultural issues, a great deal has been written about the 'ethnotheories' and 'folk' conceptions and definitions which undergird and govern the kind of care given to children around the world. My analysis takes these studies a step further by asking about the way these various cultural definitions are internalized. Without an account of the relation between culture and both body and motivational practices we may have an intuitive sense that there are culturally based strivings, but we have no explanation for how these strivings are internalized and then govern behavior in subsequent situations (D'Andrade 1992: 23). Thus it is not enough to say that 'action is culturally constituted', 'the self is culturally constituted' or 'emotion is culturally constituted' because such statements posit causal links ('x constitutes y') without specifying any kind of mechanism by which x and y might be connected (D'Andrade 1992: 41).

In this respect, however, as I showed in the chapters on sleep, play and mealtimes, when examining internalization there is a need to make an important analytical distinction: between a more 'passive' mode of gradually learning to embody certain taken-for-granted habits, and a more 'active' connection of such habits and practices to a set of incentives and inducements. This point may be underscored through the notion of group-orientation. In Chapter 4 I dealt with the question of how the 'thought-feelings' (Wikan 1989;

1991) of 'groupism' were internalized by children in Japanese preschools. The problem was to explicate the specific mechanisms by which grouping is both turned into a natural, taken-for-granted attitude to the world, and is endowed with motivational force. A number of such mechanisms work through the experiences the children undergo in preschool.

On the one hand, the concept of 'embodiment' – especially the intersubjective element involved in body practices – illuminates how group life in the sense of ways of attending to groups become transparent dispositions to the children. These body practices are what Connerton (1989: 102) terms 'incorporating practices': those largely traceless – in the sense of not providing evidence of their origin – patterns which are remembered by the body. Along these lines, in order to understand how children learn to acquire a sense of, and ability to, group is only possible in terms of those largely ephemeral and highly situation specific actions through which these practices are incorporated into the body. More generally, the children master grouping, perseverance, and eating and sleeping practices in an incremental and not always orderly manner. Socializ-ation often takes place through an exposure to partial experiences and images that are not always directly explicated, but that over the long-run result in the inculcation of basic behavioral patterns.

On the other hand, by helping children to differentiate their emotions and 'affix' them to specific situations and meanings, teachers strive towards endowing such schemas as that of grouping with motivational force. The discourse on emotions both context-ualizes and constitutes the motivational link between specific situations and the emotions that the children experience. Here I follow Myers who argues (within a social constructivist approach) that "emotions arise not in (presocial) subjective and private states but in the assumed context of social interaction, and that emotions mark the forms of relation that exist between a subject and the action/event of his or her world" (Myers 1988: 590). To put this insight by way of grouping, the emotions related to being and acting as a member of a group – comfortableness, ease, trust – not only emerge in the 'proper' social contexts but more crucially they mark (via the body) this relation itself.

These understandings bear much wider import for the study of Japanese preschools. A reading of previous studies reveals the extent to which their focus has been overwhelmingly on sight and to a lesser degree on hearing, smell, and touching. To a great extent, this situation reflects a wider characteristic of the social sciences which are marked by an almost total ignorance of the 'lower senses' especially smell and touch (Stoller 1989: 8). A focus on such activities as sleeping or eating may thus do much to introduce into our discussions a consideration of all of the faculties and senses in the processes labelled socialization. The introduction of these issues is important not just because it sheds light on a hitherto little explored area, but because it reveals that it is through all of the senses that the embodiment of relations is put into effect.

Lack of space precludes a longer exposition but let me furnish one example of how my analysis may further our understanding of one other activity which I have alluded to throughout the volume. A number of researchers have remarked about the ubiquity of rotating leadership/monitor roles (*tooban*) in Japanese preschools. From the institutional point of view, the *tooban* system is based on inculcating a sense of responsibility in children. These monitors are in charge of such things as leading classes in greetings, assembling children for events, participating in roll call, cleaning and preparing educational materials. Catherine Lewis (1991: 90) observes that the *tooban* system affords each child an opportunity to develop an identity as a classroom leader and an authority figure. In another essay she suggests (Lewis 1989: 144) that teachers take great pains to create an environment in which such practices emerge 'naturally' in children. Lewis' suggestion seems to be that responsibility is learnt through doing, through carrying out the rotating monitor role. Just how this 'learning by doing' turns into a natural 'fact' for the children is left unexplained. But if, along the lines of my analysis, one conceptualizes the *tooban* experience in terms of the attitudes it embodies, and in terms of the emotions it involves, the link to motivation and to the children's further willingness to take on such roles is made clearer.

Emotions, Power and Organization

An issue which underlies much of the analysis of how cultural conceptions are inculcated during socialization is one of power or the intentional promotion of certain body practices. In the context of preschools this point implies examining the organizational context of embodiment and of emotions. To be sure, the rhetoric governing the experience of preschool (Lewis 1989; Peak 1991a) may revolve around notions of enjoyableness and achievement (and these aspects do exist), but these elements should be seen as the outcome of a rather systematic organizational promotion of certain attitudes. Van Maanen and Kunda (1989; also Baily 1983), have done path breaking studies on the relations between formal organizations and what they term 'emotion work'. They suggest that a central concern for organizations is how to guarantee the involvement and commitment of members to organizational goals. As a consequence, modern organizations consciously and intentionally structure the 'lived experience' of their employees through attempting to govern their emotions: "rules governing the expression of emotions at work are an important part of the culture carried by organizational members and any attempt to manage culture is therefore also an attempt to manage emotions" (Van Maanen and Kunda 1989: 46). Being members of institutions of early childhood education, that is formal organizations, children too are open to this kind of control. But the picture Van Maanen and Kunda paint is not one of workers as robots, nor of a direct connection of stimulus and response between managerial instigation and workers' reactions. Workers, just like the children at Katsura, resist, negotiate and use irony to handle their situation (Kunda 1992: 181–88).

In Van Maanen's and Kunda's study – as in most studies of organizations – the end products of the organizations are services or goods. In more conventional industrial settings, emotions are governed (via a combination of positive incentives and negative control) in order to assure a smooth and efficient production flow. In newer, more service-centered industries like Disneyland, the emotions (and by extension the body stance and attitudes) of employees are controlled and managed so that they provide a good service. Put somewhat simply then, according to their model, the control of emotions in a given organization is carried out in order to achieve certain goals. In other words, were the model that Van Maanen and Kunda applied to institutions of early childhood education it would pertain to teachers and to the caretakers. While this is an important subject in itself (and is not the focus of this volume) there is yet another kind of control which goes on in preschools. In the case of Katsura *Hoikuen* – as in all preschools – the products themselves are socialized students, children who know how to control their emotions and bodies. Thus for the children, acting according to organizational goals and norms is both a prerequisite for acting as organizational members and the goal of the organization itself. Two points follow from a recognition of this situation.

First, on a theoretical level, an emphasis on organizational products questions a recent argument put forth by Martin (1992). Her thesis is that we are now witness to a shift in terms of conceptions from that of a mass produced body, the 'Fordist' Body, to a new idea of the body related to an era of flexible accumulation. Gone, as it were, are uniform concepts of bodies, and in their stead are new beliefs (and practices) about custom-made bodies. While such an argument mays sound provocative, any cursory review of what happens in educational systems in general, and preschools in particular, should cause us to challenge her contention. Preschools are still predicated on the logic of a large-scale production of standardized products. As O'Connor (1992: 91) states, as "state authority grows in nations, children are increasingly regarded as 'citizens' and are rationally and uniformly socialized by the state with the intention of advancing technical competence and promoting economic development. At the individual level, schools help teach obedience to impersonal authority, punctuality, and categorical conformity." As we saw in the case of Katsura *Hoikuen*, the emphasis is on the production of a rather consistent kind of child within the confines of the center.

Second, the stress on the rational and uniform socialization of children should be understood in a manner that is more complex than that proposed by Van Maanen and Kunda. Their emphasis (perhaps a result of their Goffmanesque assumptions) is on how the organizational construction of emotions is a conscious and intentional process; how it is essentially manipulative. While I agree that this aspect of emotional management is important, I think that the *implicit* and (often) *unintended* patterns of such regulation are no less important. Take the role of the peer group (the company of significant others) in imposing on the child a certain mode of relating to the world. Since the child has no "choice in the selection of his significant others, his identification with them is quasi- automatic. For the same reason, his identification with them is quasi-inevitable" (Berger and Luckmann 1967: 154). He or she, in contrast to the employees of most organizations, internalizes the world as *the* world, the only existent and conceivable world. In this manner, the power and the legitimacy of the group lie precisely in the fact that the artificial, and the socially constructed nature of group affiliation is not shown.

What does this point imply? Through the various activities of the preschool (such as the daily timetable or group activities) the children learn to be organization men and women in the sense of embodying certain attitudes and stances. Lock (1983: following Comaroff and Comaroff 1991) distinguishes between agentive forms of power in which authoritative control is exerted directly over others and nonagentive forms in which power proliferates outside the direct realm of institutional politics to saturate such things as aesthetics, bodily regimentation, medical knowledge and mundane usage. Nonagentive power becomes internalized as part of a cultural repertoire that may be experienced in many ways: negatively as constraints, neutrally as conventions, or positively as values. The nonagentive power of preschools is thus related to preparing children for the future (a point I return to presently) not only by granting them the basic abilities to fulfill social roles, but by governing the manner in which they adjust to certain organized routine and practices. Thus, hegemony is quite literally, as Bourdieu and others show, 'habit forming' (Lock 1993: 68).

But saying that the children learn to 'embody' the organization (and the power relations it predicates) is still not enough because there remains the need to specify the mechanisms through which this embodiment is effected. While I have dealt with a number of such mechanisms in previous chapters, let me provide another instance which illuminates the relations between organization, embodiment and power: organizational time reckoning. Clock time is concretized in industrial societies into the body in a way that fuses with body time; and then back into the visible 'object' world of clocks and bells and schedules and timetables of the order of industry and workplace. "Clock time is not lifeless but quite alive, embodied in purposeful activity and experience. Coordinately, people are ongoingly articulated through this temporization into a wider politico-cosmic order, a world time of particular values and powers" (Munn 1992). Munn's point is that when time 'enters' the body it does so with it all the meticulous controls of power: the body is not only the fundamental means of tacit temporization, but is also part of the means for constant movement back and forth between self and world.

In terms of preschools, two points follow this postulate. First, such institutions are the first formal organizations in which children encounter the systematic use of time-reckoning and the arrangement and coordination of relatively large-scale activities on the basis of this reckoning. In this way, the children are implicitly prepared for the workplace by embodying personal time *and* organizational time. To put this point by way of example, the individual bodily rhythms of sleeping and eating are gradually synchronized with the tempos of the preschool in a manner that the children experience as natural. Second, we must be wary of reducing everything to a harsh kind of discipline. Within preschools, the children are not only controlled but also come to feel comfortable in the parameters of such time reckoning.[1] And, it is this essential comfortableness – implicit, unreflective, mundane – which under-girds the power of the institution. Toren's (1993: 464) conclusions are apt in this regard. She posits that the meaning of various public events is "cognitively coercive in so far as the process by which we come to constitute its meaning is obscure to us". This situation ensues because the "affective dimension of concepts tends to be carried in the body itself and what we convey through bodily praxis is for the most part outside our own conscious awareness or control and outside the conscious awareness of those who observe us" (Toren 1993: 466)

This kind of theoretical approach furthers our understanding of many insights found in the literature on Japanese preschools. Peak (1991a: 76), for example, states that the main curriculum of Japanese preschools is contained in the structure and routine of the school day itself. The objectives of preschool "are not accomplished through carefully planned curriculum units or extensive correction and disciplining of inappropriate behavior. Rather, they are nurtured through a gradual process of socialization in group routines and the inculcation of habits conducive to group life. The expectations and demands of the daily schedule and its attendant ritual are the main vehicle of instruction in this process". While Peak does not make her theoretical assumption clear, I would suggest that her insight is grounded in a premise that the children gradually learn to embody the educational goals of preschools. Furthermore, my point is that the schedule is part of industrial or complex bureaucratic time, and the implicit adaptation of children is not only to group life, but to group life in organizations. The very naturalness of organizational timetables – and by extension other kinds of organizational arrangements – gradually come to penetrate the very core of the children's subjectivity.

Future Behavior: Key Scenarios

What are the long-term effects of preschools? What are the relations between such institutions and adult behavior? Rohlen (1989b: 5) cautions that while we should not be dissuaded "from attempting to identify the basic underlying processes that distinguish the way order is formed in Japanese society", but that by looking for the links between childhood and adulthood we may create a misleading impression of uniformity and monocausality. Theoretically speaking, we are led back to the issues raised by the grand 'culture and personality' school of the early post World War II era. The school – represented in Japan formostly by Ruth Benedict (1946) – contended that a society's characteristic childrearing techniques produced national cultural forms, including basic personality constellations. Parents and kinsmen were thought of as being the primary producers of this national culture (Fox 1990). Today, however, this conceptualization has changed: national culture "does not have the hard, fully formed, or configured quality attributed to it by the anthropology of two generations ago . . . For us, national culture is malleable and mobile. It is the outcome of a constant process of cultural production. A national culture is constantly being molded as individuals and groups confront their social worlds and try to (re)form them" (Fox 1990: 2). Within Japanese studies, this latter approach has been taken up by such scholars as Robertson (1992), Bestor (1992) and on a more micro level by Bachnik (1994) and Rosenberger (1992). Such scholars have put the accent on the essential negotiability, contestation and lability of Japanese culture.

Such an approach raises a question about the implication of viewing culture as contested and negotiable for the relation between childhood patterns of socialization and adult behavior. Essentially, the question is how to conceptualize, at one and the same time, the continuities between these two periods and the openness of cultural constructs. As I suggested earlier, the notions of 'key scenarios', 'scripts' or 'schemas' in Japanese culture may aid us in this respect. 'Key scenarios' according to Ortner (1973) are valued because they formulate a culture's basic means-ends relationships in actable forms. They may be formal, usually named events, or sequences of action that are enacted and reenacted according to unarticulated formulae in the normal course of everyday events. In related parlance, a 'script' or 'schema' is a distinct and strongly interconnected pattern of interpretive elements which can be activated with minimum inputs. A schema is an interpretation which is frequent, well organized, memorable, which can be made from minimal cues, contains one or more prototypic instantiations and is relatively resistant to change (D'Andrade 1992: 29). The importance of this conceptualization is threefold: it goes beyond the stress on values and attitudes to put at the center of attention the actable forms which people learn; it shows that not much has to be done (minimal cues) for these actable forms to be actualized by people; and it allows the notion of body to come in via the place of comfortableness and learnt practices that people gradually learn to inhabit.

For example, as I proposed in Chapter 3, co-sleeping is a "key scenario" in Japanese culture. This scenario is valued because it formulates one of Japanese culture's basic notions of grouping in an actable form. If we conceptualize forms like co-sleeping as scenarios that Japanese people learn to 'carry in their heads' as well as 'carry in their bodies', we can understand how these schemas can be activated in a variety of contexts throughout their life course. What my interpretation clarifies is the place of accumulated experience (pre-adaption) in compelling people to carry out these key scenarios: through co-sleeping with his or her peer group during childhood, the adult Japanese has learnt to embody the experience of grouping in an intimate manner.

It is in a similar vein that other scenarios learnt at preschool should be seen: co-eating and drinking, cooperative play, entry and graduation ceremonies or sports field-days. All of these scenarios, which are played out along the life course, have a number of concrete implications.[2] The first is a situation in which when children (and later adults) enter one of these organizational forms, they can orient themselves with little fumbling about and little wastage of organizational resources (such as time and attention); these scenarios are not allusions or abstract principles, but are made up of prescriptions for concrete actions and techniques which individuals may use. People implicitly know how to act. They have internalized the knowledge, the motivation and the comfortableness to act within these scenarios. With time, all of these scenarios become native models that are available culturally to all (middle-class) Japanese. The theoretical point here is that there is an efficiency inherent in 'scripted knowledge': the use of scripts for oft-repeated encounters frees the individual's attention for other things (Light 1987: 56).

Let me clarify this idea again through group-orientation. "The Japanese preschool prepares children for the group life they will encounter in elementary school, junior high and beyond by giving children many opportunities to participate in both formal, cere- monial, highly structured (*omote*) group activities led by teachers and in informal, unstructured, spontaneous (*ura*) group activities" (Tobin 1992: 32). The point is that this process cannot be under- stood only through a learning model. What I offer here is a model that integrates into one theoretical framework elements of motivation, habit, and the automaticity of natural behavior in group contexts. This framework does not mean that such scenarios are not used intentionally by Japanese people to further their own ends. It does, however, underline how the scenarios are inter- nalized and how they are often used or mobilized without much conscious attention.

This aspect is best exemplified through various dimensions of behavior involved in *gambaru*. Persistence, is should be stressed, includes both a volitional aspect centering on action and a dispo- sitional one focused on the constraints of the body. To take off from Turner (1992: 95), the children learn to handle both the 'body as constraint' and 'the body as capacity'. In this sense we go beyond Bourdieu (see Turner 1992: 91) whose emphasis on habitus is deterministic: a system of dispositions with reference to a given place which produce regularities in modes of behavior. In his rendering, the body is primarily a bearer of certain cultural codes. But as I argue, the purposeful and conscious aspects of action should also be brought into our analysis: *gambaru* also involves innovation, application to new situations and is linked to children's intentions.

Children and 'Politics': Power and the 'Self'

The model I have been proposing here posits elements of both negotiability and continuity; it revolves around a notion of internal- izing a set of scenarios which can be intentionally and innovatively used by individuals to further their (personal or collective) aims throughout the life-course. An approach which integrates ideas of negotiation, choice and agency into a model of social life is by now quite commonplace within the social sciences. But I would posit that it has become a standard one primarily in regard to adults, to grown-up members of cultures. The problem is that many of the models related to childhood practices still proceed from the assumption of the relative passivity, immaturity and dependency of children. As I suggested in Chapter 7, we may benefit from treating children as political problems (from an adult's point of view) (Waksler 1986: 74), or (better still) as political actors with at least some power to resist and change the circumstances within which they live. Such a model would help us examine such issues related to childhood as bargaining and coalition building, the power of the weak, collective goals, creating factions and rehearsals for leadership.

Take the criticisms, irony, obscenity, and name-calling that I have outlined in the previous chapter. They may violate certain academic notions of Japanese children, but their sheer ubiquity and dynamism underscore how central they are to the ways in which youngsters relate to their lives. To paraphrase Helen Schwartzman (1978: 12), teachers and educators (and most of the 'experts' they depend on) tend to view such play behavior in terms of what it is not: not work, not real, not serious, not productive and not contributive. My contention is that much of our social scientific understanding of socialization in general, and in Japan in particular, has adopted this view of critical play. Indeed, these assumptions underscore the idea that both the preschool and the workplace are essentially similar sites where serious and productive work is undertaken. In contrast, my argument is that acts of caprice and questioning should be seen as constitutive of preschools to the same degree as their formal organizational hierarchy, division of labor and curriculum.

This point is directly related to whom we listen to in our studies. Holland (cited in D'Andrade 1992: 39) states that "much ethnographic work is slanted toward the expert's culture". In explicating cultural knowledge and practices we depict "a level of expertise, a level of salience, and a level of identification that may in fact be appropriate only for describing a small subset of the people studied". We may benefit then, not only from asking the experts, but also the children themselves. Rather than asking only the people in power who are usually most vocal and eloquent we may benefit from asking others.

A political model of preschools has another implication that is not always associated with politics. My proposition is that such a model intimates a different conceptualization of the socialization of selves in Japan. Let me put this by way of a question: if we allow that the children are independent social actors – that is, they have a will of their own, are able to independently appraise situations and rationally pursue their aims – then what are the implications of this view for the manner by which we conceptualize their internal strengths? Take the long-term effects of 'mischief'. By these effects I do not mean the standard view which sees early childhood education as preparing children for the rigors of school and the workplace. Nor do I refer to Tobin, Wu and Davidson's stress on 'developmentally appropriate chaos' through which the children learn to differentiate between the behaviors suitable to different situations. Rather, I would argue that the long-term effect of critical play can be understood in terms of the capacity an individual develops to distance herself or himself from highly committed social situations; to develop what Erving Goffman terms 'role distance'. In discussing the 'typical' worker in Japanese organizations, Plath (1983: 9) notes:

> He may be loyal to the organization, he may serve it with diligence. This does not mean he deposits his mind in the company safe. He must maintain a healthy detachment, sustain a sense of personal continuity among what he is likely, in his organizational role, to experience as a planless tangle of reassignment and delays.

I suggest that the ability to disengage oneself from ongoing organizational (or more generally social) life which is found among many Japanese workers begins to be acquired in preschool through the playful behaviors I have been examining. The capacity for detachment – not always fully conscious, often mixed with humor – thus seems to be no less important for survival in companies and bureaucracies than other traits as perseverance, powers of concentration and the ability to work in a group (see for example Kondo 1990: 212–3). Along these lines, while behaviors as name-calling are adaptive to the workplace, their adaptive value is an *unintended consequence* of what is understood by the participants (and especially by the teachers) to be 'not serious'.

This point bears much wider theoretical import in the context of Japanese studies. Within the scholarly study of Japan, the main stress has been on the strong group and interpersonal ties which bind people together (Benedict 1946; Smith 1983; Nakane 1973). Thus, in a thorough review of the literature on cross-cultural concepts of the self, Markus and Kitayama (1991: 33) state that

"Japanese emotions (like those of other people's with 'interdependent' selves) are 'other-focused' – that is, they 'have another person, rather than one's own internal attributes, as the primary referent.' Hence, they argue, compared with people with 'independent' selves, Japanese individuals are much more sensitive to others, more often take the perspective of others, and are concerned to further cooperative or altruistic social behavior. The image that emerges from this conclusion is one of individuals who are bound in strong social bonds to others and therefore show a relative lack of personal autonomy.

But a closer examination of this conclusion reveals a more complex picture. Hollan (1992: 6–7) notes that while "cultural and linguistic categories . . . provide one important means by which the self is conceptualized – and talked about – it is nevertheless the case that cultural models and conceptions of the self should not be conflated with the experiential self per se". We must not *assume* that "cultural conceptions of the self are isomorphic not only with the actors' conceptions of the self, but with their mental representation of their own self as well" (Spiro 1993: 119). To follow Ewing (1991: 137), if interpersonal autonomy is distinguished from intrapsychic, then there is no convincing reason to believe that the Japanese (or members of other socio-centric cultures) are any less characterized by intrapsychic autonomy than Americans are. My point is that the roots of this autonomy are found in various patterns of early childhood socialization: the long-term effects of such activities as critical play are of fostering intrapsychic autonomy. To reiterate, while there may be relatively little interpersonal autonomy in many Japanese situations, this does not imply a lack of intrapersonal independence.

My last point is related to another assumption that marks many studies of socialization in Japan. The goal of most such studies (including some of my own) is to explain how social systems maintain sameness (Schwartzman 1978: 99). This assumption is evident in the questions we ask: for instance, how is a culture transmitted from one generation to the next. In asking such a question, we assume that Japanese culture is a kind of static entity that can be transferred wholesale from one point in time to another. Newer approaches (Bachnik 1994) stress the constant negotiability that marks Japanese (as any other) culture. In these approaches however, the basic parameters – such as the *uchi/soto* distinction – are given and people negotiate about how to actualize them in specific situations. But if our goal is also to explain how social systems generate difference, then a focus on the clowning and mischief – and the manner in which they interconnect, intersect and constantly question different meaning structures (Babcock 1984: 108) – may be useful. In other words, because the power of critical play to recreate reality and to reinvent culture lies in the novelty of forms it gives rise to, this may ultimately be its most significant role. It may well be that future studies of early childhood socialization will turn to sources' of cultural innovation.

Notes

1 In a cross-cultural study, Friedman (1990: 111–3) found that in all industrial societies, people tend to experience time as a kind of pressure to be punctual and to be busy. He also found that, comparatively speaking, the Japanese tend to show greatest time pressure (as measured, for example, in the accuracy of bank clocks, the average duration of a bank transaction and in the pace of walking in the street). While I could not find any comparable data on preschools in other societies, it could be suggested that one source of the stress on time reckoning and pressure in Japan is the experience of time in institutions of early childhood education.

2 For example sports days are held in a variety of settings such as schools (Dore 1978: 179), neighborhoods and villages (Brown 1979: 25; Hendry 1981: 70), and companies (Dore 1973: 205; Rohlen 1974: 110–11).

References

Abu-Lughod, Lila and Catherine A. Lutz 1990: Introduction: Emotion, Discourse and the Politics of Everyday Life. In Catherine A. Lutz and Lila Abu-Lughod (eds.): *Language and the Politics of Emotion*. Pp. 1–23. Cambridge: Cambridge University Press.

Amanuma, Kaoru 1987: *Gambari no Kozo: Nihonjin no Kodo Genri*. Tokyo: Yoshikawa Kobunkan.

Ashkenazi, Michael 1990: Anthropological Aspects of the Japanese Meal: Tradition, Internationalization, and Aesthetics. In Adriana Boscaro, Franco Gatti and Massimo Raveri (eds.): *Rethinking Japan*. Vol II. Pp. 338–49. Sandgate, Kent: Japan Library Limited.

Atkinson, Paul 1984; Eating Virtue. In Anne Murcott (ed.): *The Sociology of Food and Eating*. Pp. 9–17. London: Gower.

Aubert, V. and H. White 1959: Sleep: A Sociological Interpretation. *Acta Sociologica* 4(1): 46–54; 4(2): 1–16.

Babcock, Barbara A. 1984: Arrange Me into Disorder: Fragments and Reflections on Ritual Clowning. In John J. MacAloon (ed.): *Rite, Drama, Festival, Spectacle: Rehearsals Toward a Theory of Cultural Performance*. Pp. 102–25. Philadelphia: Institute for the Study of Human Issues.

Bachnik, Jane M. 1992: The Two 'Faces' of Self and Society in Japan. *Ethos* 20(1): 3–32.

Bachnik, Jane M. 1994: Introduction: *Uchi/Soto*: Challenging Our Conceptualizations of Self, Social Order, and Language. In Jane M. Bachnik and Charles J. Quinn Jr. (eds.): *Situated Meanings: Inside and Outside in Japanese Self, Society, and Language*. Pp. 3–37. Princeton: Princeton University Press.

Bachnik, Jane M.and Charles J. Quinn Jr. (eds.) 1994: *Situated Meanings: Inside and Outside in Japanese Self, Society, and Language*. Princeton: Princeton University Press.

Backhouse, Anthony E. 1976: How to Remember Numbers in Japanese. In Barbara Kirshenblatt-Gimblett, (ed.): *Speech Play*. Pp. 149–61. Philadelphia: University of Pennsylvania Press.

Baily, Fredrick G. 1983: *The Tactical Uses of Passion*. Ithaca: Cornell University Press.

Bateson, Gregory 1972: *Steps Toward and Ecology of Mind*. New York: Ballantine.

Bateson, Mary Catherine 1991: *Our Own Metaphor*. Washington, D.C.: Smithsonian Institution Press.

Befu, Harumi 1971: *Japan: An Anthropological Introduction*. San Francisco: Chandler.

Ben-Ari, Eyal 1986: A Sports Day in Suburban Japan: Leisure, Artificial Communities and the Creation of Local Sentiments. In Joy Hendry and Jonathan Webber (eds.): *Interpreting Japanese Society: Anthropological Approaches*. Pp. 211–25. Oxford: JASO Occasional Papers No. 5.

Ben-Ari, Eyal 1987: Disputing about Day-Care: Care-Taking Roles in a Japanese Day Nursery. *International Journal of Sociology of the Family* 17: 197–216.

Ben-Ari, Eyal 1989: At the Interstices: Drinking, Management and Temporary Groups in a Local Japanese Organization. *Social Analysis* 26: 46–64.

Ben-Ari, Eyal 1991: *Changing Japanese Suburbia: A Study of Two Present-Day Localities*. London: Kegan Paul International.

Ben-Ari, Eyal 1993: *Sake and 'Spare Time': Management and Imbibement in Japanese Business Firms*. Papers in Japanese Studies No. 18. National University of Singapore: Department of Japanese Studies.

Ben-Ari, Eyal 1995: Caretaking with a Pen. *International Journal of Comparative Sociology* 24(2): 31–48.

Ben-Ari Eyal (forthcoming) *Organization and Culture in Japanese Childcare: An Interpretive Study*. London: Kegan Paul International.

Benedict, Ruth 1946: *The Chrysanthemum and the Sword*. Boston: Houghton Mifflin.

Berger, Peter L. and Thomas Luckmann 1967: *The Social Construction of Reality*. Harmondsworth: Penguin.

Bestor, Theodore 1992: Conflict, Legitimacy, and Tradition in a Tokyo Neighborhood. In Takie S. Lebra (ed.): *Japanese Social Organization*. Pp. 23–47. Honolulu: University of Hawaii Press.

Bethel, Diana Lynn 1992: Life in Obasuteyama or, Inside a Japanese Institution for the Elderly. In Takie S. Lebra (ed.): *Japanese Social Organization*. Pp. 109–34. Honolulu: University of Hawaii Press.

Bettleheim, Ruth and Ruby Takanishi 1976: *Early Schooling in Asia*. New York: McGraw-Hill.

Blacking, John 1977: Towards and Anthropology of the Body. In John Blacking (ed.): *The Anthropology of the Body*. Pp. 1–28. London: Academic Press.

Boocock, Saranne S. 1977: A Crosscultural Analysis of the Childcare System. In L.G. Katz et. al. (eds.): *Current Topics in Early Childhood Education*. Vol. 1. Pp. 71–103. Norwood, N.J.: Ablex.

Boocock, Saranne S. 1989: Controlled Diversity: An Overview of the Japanese Preschool System. *Journal of Japanese Studies* 15(1): 41–68.

Bourdieu, Pierre 1977: *Outline of a Theory of Practice*. Cambridge: Cambridge University Press.

Brinkman, Wilhelm 1986: The Metamorphosis of Childhood: Thoughts on its Emergence and Disappearance, and its Importance for Educational Theory. *Education* 33: 78–93.

Brown, Keith 1979: Introduction. In his (trans.) *Shingo: The Chronicle of a Japanese Village*. University Center for International Studies, Ethnology Monographs No. 2. University of Pittsburgh.

Bruner, Jerome 1986: *Actual Minds, Possible Worlds*. Cambridge, Mass.: Harvard University Press.

Carney, Larry S. and Charlotte G. O'Kelly 1990: Women's Work and Women's Place in the Japanese Economic Miracle. In Kathryn Ward (ed.): *Women Workers and Global Restructuring*. Pp. 113–45. Cornell International Industrial and Labor Relations Report Number 17. ILR Press.

Caudill, William and David W. Plath 1986: Who Sleeps by Whom? Parent-Child Involvement in Urban Japanese Families. In Takie S. Lebra and William P. Lebra (eds.): *Japanese Culture and Behavior: Selected Readings*. Pp. 247–79. Honolulu: University of Hawaii Press.

Caudill, William and Helen Weinstein 1969: Maternal Care and Infant Behavior in Japan and America. *Psychiatry* 32: 12–43.

Charles, Nickie and Marion Kerr 1988: *Women, Food and Families*. Manchester: Manchester University Press.

Coleman, Samuel 1983: *Family Planning in Japanese Society: Traditional Birth Control in a Modern Urban Culture*. Princeton: Princeton University Press.

Comaroff, John and Jean Comaroff 1991: *Ethnography and the Historical Imagination*. Boulder: Westview.

Connerton, Paul 1989: *How Societies Remember*. Cambridge: Cambridge University Press.

Conroy, Mary, Robert D. Hess, Hiroshi Azuma, and Keiko Kashiwagi 1980: Maternal Strategies for Regulating Children's Behavior: Japanese and American Families. *Journal of Cross-Cultural Psychology* 11(2): 153–72.

Corsaro, William M. 1988: Routines in the Peer Culture of American and Italian Nursery School Children. *Sociology of Education* 61: 1–14.

Creighton, Millie R. 1990: Revisiting Shame and Guilt Cultures: A Forty Year Pilgrimage. *Ethos* 18: 279–307.

Csikszentmihalyi, Mihaly 1975: *Beyond Boredom and Anxiety*. San Francisco: Jossey-Bass.

Csikszentmihalyi, Mihaly and Ronald Graef 1975: Socialization into Sleep: Exploratory Findings. *Merrill-Palmer Quarterly* 21(1): 3–18.

Csordas, Thomas J. 1993: Somatic Modes of Attention, *Cultural Anthropology* 8(2): 135–56.

Cummings, William 1980: *Education and Equality in Japan*. Princeton: Princeton University Press.

D'Andrade, Roy G. 1992: Schemas and Motivation. In Roy G. D'Andrade and Claudia Strauss (eds.): *Human Motives and Cultural Models*. Pp. 23–44. Cambridge: Cambridge University Press.

DeCoker, Gary 1989: Japanese Preschools: Academic or Nonacademic? In James J. Shields, Jr. (ed.): *Japanese Schooling: Patterns of Socialization, Equality, and Political Control*. Pp. 45–58. University Park: Pennsylvania State University Press.

Denzin, Norman 1977: *Childhood Socialization.* San Francisco: Jossey-Bass.

De Vos, George 1973: *Socialization for Achievement.* Berkeley: University of California Press.

De Vos, George 1986: The Relation of Guilt Toward Parents to Achievement and Arranged Marriage Among the Japanese. In Takie S. and William P. Lebra (eds.): *Japanese Culture and Behavior.* Pp. 80–101. Honolulu: University of Hawaii Press.

Doi, Takeo 1973: *The Anatomy of Dependence.* Tokyo: Kodansha.

Dore, Ronald 1958: *City Life in Japan.* Berkeley: University of California Press.

Dore, Ronald 1973: *British Factory, Japanese Factory.* Berkeley: University of California Press.

Dore, Ronald 1978: *Shinohata: A Portrait of a Japanese Village.* London: Allen Lane.

Douglas, Mary 1984: Standard Social Uses of Food: Introduction. In Mary Douglas (ed.): *Food in the Social Order.* Pp. 1–39. New York: Russell Sage Foundation.

Early Childhood Education Association of Japan 1979: *Childhood Education and Care in Japan.* Tokyo: Child Honsha.

Elias, Norbert 1978: *The Civilizing Process Volume I: The History of Manners.* New York: Pantheon.

Edwards, Walter 1989: *Modern Japan Through its Weddings: Gender, Person, and Society in Ritual Portrayal.* Stanford: Stanford University Press.

Ewing, Katherine P. 1990: The Illusion of Wholeness: Culture, Self, and the Experience of Inconsistency. *Ethos* 18: 251–78.

Featherstone, Mike 1991: The Body in Consumer Culture. In Mike Featherstone, Mike Hepworth and Bryan S. Turner (eds.): *The Body: Social Processes and Cultural Theory.* Pp. 170–96. London: Sage.

Fiddes, Nick 1991: *Meat: A Natural Symbol.* London: Routledge.

Fine, Gary A. 1988: Good Children and Dirty Play. *Play and Culture* 1: 43–56.

Friedman, William 1990: *About Time: Inventing the Fourth Dimension.* Cambridge, Mass.: MIT Press.

Foucault, Michel 1979: *Discipline and Punish: The Birth of the Prison.* New York: Vintage.

Foucault, Michel 1980: *The History of Sexuality: Vol. I, An Introduction.* New York: Vintage.

Fox, Richard G. 1990: Introduction. In Richard G. Fox (ed.): *Nationalist Ideologies and the Production of National Cultures.* Pp. 1–14. Washington D.C. (American Anthropological Association): American Ethnological Society Monograph Series Number 2.

Fratto, Toni F. 1976: Jesters: Reflections on Anthropology and *Human Nature.* Anthropologica 18: 53–63.

Fruehstueck, Sabine 1994: 'Body Projects' in Contemporary Japan. Paper presented at a conference of the European Association of Japanese Studies. Copenhagen, August.

Fujita, Mariko 1989: 'It's All Mother's Fault': Childcare and Socialization of Working Mothers in Japan. *Journal of Japanese Studies* 15(1): 67–92.

Fujita, Mariko and Toshiyuki Sano 1988: Children in American and Japanese Day-Care Centers: Ethnography and Reflective Cross-Cultural Interviewing. In Henry T.Treuba and Concha Delgado-Gaitan (eds.): *School and Society: Learning Through Culture*. Pp. 73–97. New York: Plenum.

Fuller, Bruce, Susan D. Holloway, Hiroshi Azuma, Robert D. Hess, and Keiko Kashiwagi 1986: Contrasting Achievement Rules: Socialization of Japanese at Home and in School. *Research in Sociology of Education* 6: 165–201.

Gerbert, Elaine 1993: Lessons form the *Kokugo* (National Language) Readers. *Comparative Education Review* 37(2) 152–80.

Geertz, Clifford 1983: *Local Knowledge: Further Essays in Interpretive Anthropology*. New York: Basic Books.

Goody, Jack 1977:1977: *The Domestication of the Savage Mind*. Cambridge: Cambridge University Press.

Goody, Jack 1982: *Cooking, Cuisine and Class: A Study in Comparative Sociology*. Cambridge: Cambridge University Press.

Greif, Esther B. 1977: Peer Interactions in Preschool Children. In Roger A. Webb (ed.): *Social Development in Childhood: Day-Care Programs Research*. Pp. 141–60. Baltimore: Johns Hopkins University Press.

Handelman, Don 1981: Introduction: The Idea of Bureaucratic Organization. *Social Analysis* 9: 5–23.

Harkness, Sara and Charles M. Super 1983: The Cultural Construction of Child Development: A Framework for the Socialization of Affect. *Ethos* 11(4): 221–31.

Hayashi, Hiroko 1985: Japan. In J. Farley (ed.): *Women Workers in Fifteen Countries*. Pp. 57–63. Ithaca: JLR Press.

Hendry Joy 1981: *Marriage in Changing Japan: Community and Society*. London: Croom Helm.

Hendry, Joy 1984: Becoming Japanese: A Social Anthropological View of Childrearing. *Journal of the Anthropological Society of Oxford* 15(2): 101–18.

Hendry, Joy 1986a: *Becoming Japanese: The World of the Pre-School Child*. Manchester: Manchester University Press.

Hendry, Joy 1986b: Kindergartens and the Transition from Home to School Education. *Comparative Education* 22(1): 53–8.

Hess, Robert D., Keiko Kashiwagi, Hiroshi Azuma, Gary G. Price, and W. Patrick Dickson 1980: Maternal Expectations for Mastery of Developmental Tasks in Japan and the United States. *International Journal of Psychology* 15: 259–71.

Hobbs, Nicholas 1975: *The Futures of Children*. San Francisco: Jossey-Bass.

Hollan, Douglas 1992: Cross-Cultural Differences in the Self. *Journal of Anthropological Research* 48: 283–300.

Holland, Dorothy and Andrew Kipnis 1994: Metaphors for Embarrassment and Stories of Exposure: The Not-So-Egocentric Self in American Culture. *Ethos* 22(3): 316–42.

Ikegame, Mieko 1982: *Sisters of the Sun: Japanese Women Today*. London: Change International Reports: Women and Society.

Ishigaki, Emiko H. 1987: A Comparison of Young Children's Environments and Parental Expectations in Japan and Israel. *Early Child Development and Care* 27: 139–68.

Ivy, Marilyn 1989: Critical Texts, Mass Artifacts: The Consumption of Knowledge in Postmodern Japan. In Masao Miyoshi and H.D. Harootunian (eds.): *Postmodernism and Japan*. Pp. 21–46. Durham: Duke University Press.

Kelly, William W. 1991: Directions in the Anthropology of Contemporary Japan. *Annual Review of Anthropology* 20: 395–431.

Kirshenblatt-Gimblett, Barbara and Joel Sherzer 1976: Introduction. In Barbara Kirshenblatt-Gimblett, (ed.): Speech Play. Pp. 1–18. Philadelphia: University of Pennsylvania Press.

Kishima, Takako 1991: *Political Life in Japan: Democracy in a Reversible World*. Princeton: Princeton University Press.

Kojima, Hideo 1986: Childrearing Concepts as a Belief-Value System of the Society and the Individual. In Harold Stevenson *et al.* (eds.): *Child Development and Education in Japan*. Pp. 39–54. New York: W.H. Freeman.

Kondo, Dorinne 1990: *Crafting Selves: Power, Gender and Discourses of Identity in a Japanese Workplace*. Chicago: Chicago University Press.

Kondo, Dorinne 1992: Multiple Selves: The Aesthetics and Politics of Artisanal Identities. In Nancy R. Rosenberger (ed.): *Japanese Sense of Self*. Pp. 40–66. Cambridge: Cambridge University Press.

Koschmann, J. Victor 1978: Introduction: Soft Rule and Expressive Protest. In J. Victor Koschmann (ed.); *Authority and the Individual in Japan*. Pp. 1–30. Tokyo: Tokyo University Press.

Koseisho 1993: *Kosei Hakusho*. Tokyo: Koseisho.

Kotloff, Lauren J. 1988: *Dai-Ichi Preschool: Fostering Individuality and Cooperative Group Life in a Progressive Japanese Preschool*. Ph.D. Thesis, Cornell University.

Kumagai, Hisa A. 1981: A Dissection of Intimacy: A Study of 'Bipolar Posturing' in Japanese Social Interaction – *Amaeru* and *Amayakasu*, Indulgence and Deference. *Culture, Medicine and Psychiatry* 5: 249–72.

Kumon, Shimpei 1982: Some Principles Governing the Thought and Behavior of Japanists (Contextualists). *Journal of Japanese Studies* 7(1): 5–29.

Kunda, Gideon 1992: *Engineering Culture: Control and Commitment in a High-Tech Corporation*. Philadelphia: Temple University Press.

Lanham, Betty B. 1966: The Psychological Orientation of the Mother-Child Relationship in Japan. *Monumenta Nipponica* 21: 322–33.

Lanham, Betty B. 1986: Ethics and Moral Precepts Taught in Schools of Japan and the United States. In Takie S. Lebra (ed.): *Japanese Culture and Behavior*. Pp. 280–96. Honolulu: University of Hawaii Press.

Lavie, Peretz 1991: The 24-Hour Sleep Propensity Function (SPF): Practical and Theoretical Implications. In Timothy H. Monk (ed.): *Sleep, Sleepiness and Performance*. Pp. 65–93. Chichester: J. Wiley.

Lebra, Joyce 1976: Conclusions. In Joyce Lebra, J. Paulson and E. Powers (eds.): *Women in Changing Japan*. Pp. 297–304. Stanford: Stanford University Press.

Lebra, Takie S. 1976: *Japanese Patterns of Behavior.* Honolulu: University of Hawaii Press.

Lebra, Takie S. 1984: *Japanese Women: Constraint and Fulfillment.* Honolulu: University of Hawaii Press.

Lebra, Takie S. 1995 Skipped and Postponed Adolescence of Aristocratic Women in Japan: Resurrecting the Culture/Nature Issue. *Ethos* 23(1): 79–102.

Lewis, Catherine 1989: From Indulgence to Internalization: Social Control in the Early School Years. *Journal of Japanese Studies* 15(1): 139–57.

Lewis, Catherine 1991: Nursery Schools: The Transition from Home to School. In Barbara Finkelstein, Anne E. Imamura, and Joseph Tobin (eds.): *Transcending Stereotypes: Discovering Japanese Culture and Education.* Pp. 81–95. Yarmouth, Maine: Intercultural Press.

Lewis, Catherine 1993: Review of Lois Peak: Learning to Go to School in Japan. *Journal of Japanese Studies* Vol. 19 (book review section).

Light, Paul 1987: Taking Roles. In Jerome Bruner and Helen Haste (eds.): *Making Sense: The Child's Construction of the World.* Pp. 41–61. London: Methuen.

Lock, Margaret M. 1987: Introduction: Health and Medical Care as Cultural and Social Phenomena. In Edward Norbeck and Margaret Lock (eds.): *Health, Illness and Medical Care in Japan.* Pp. 1–23. Honolulu: University of Hawaii Press.

Lock, Margaret M. 1993: Cultivating the Body: Anthropology and Epistemologies of Bodily Practice and Knowledge. *Annual Review of Anthropology* 22: 133–55.

Lupri, Eugen 1983: The Changing Position of Women and Men in Comparative Perspective. In Eugen Lupri (ed.): *The Changing Position of Women in Family and Society.* Pp. 3–39. Leiden: E.J. Brill.

Lutz, Catherine 1985: Ethnopsychology Compared to What? Explaining Behavior and Consciousness among the Ifaluk. In G.M. White and J. Kirkpatrick (eds.): *Pacific Ethnopsychologies.* Pp. 35–79. Berkeley: University of California Press.

Lutz, Catherine 1987: Goals, Events, and Understanding in Ifaluk Emotion Theory. In Dorothy Holland and Naomi Quinn (eds.): *Cultural Models in Language and Thought.* Pp. 290–312. Cambridge: Cambridge University Press.

Lutz, Catherine A. 1988 *Unnatural Emotions: Everyday Sentiments on a Micronesian Atoll and Their Challenge to Western Theory.* Chicago: University of Chicago Press.

Mackay, Robert W. 1974: Conceptions of Childhood and Models of Socialization. In Roy Turner (ed.) *Ethnomethodology.* Pp. 180–93. London: Penguin.

Markus, Hazel R. and Shinobu Kitayama 1991: Culture and the Self: Implications for Cognition, Emotion, and Motivation. *Psychological Review* 98(2): 224–53.

Martin, Emily 1992: The End of the Body? *American Ethnologist* 19(1): 121–40.

Martinez, D.l. 1990: Tourism and the Ama: The Search for a Real Japan. In Eyal Ben-Ari, Brian Moeran, and James Valentine (eds.): *Unwrapping Japan.* Pp. 97–116. Manchester: Manchester University Press.

Matsumoto, Y. Scott 1970: Social Stress and Coronary Heart Disease in Japan: A Hypothesis. *Milbank Memorial Fund Quarterly*, 63: 9–36.

Mayer, Karl Ulrich and Walter Muller 1986: The State and the Structure of the Life Course. In A.B. Sorenson (ed): *Human Development and the Life Course*, Pp. 217–45. Boston: Earlbaum.

McVeigh, Brian 1991: Gratitude, Obedience, and the Humility of Heart: The Morality of Dependency in a New Religion. *The Journal of Social Science* (International Christian University) 30(2): 107–25.

McVeigh, Brian 1993: Building Belief Through the Body: The Physical Embodiment of Morality and Doctrine in Sukyo Mahikari. *Japanese Religions* 18(2): 140–61.

McVeigh, Brian 1994: Engendering Gender Through the Body: Learning to be an 'Office Lady' at a Japanese Women's Junior College. Manuscript submitted for review.

Mechling, Jay 1986: Children's Folklore. In Elliot Oring (ed): Pp. 91–120. Logan, Utah: Utah State University Press.

Mennell, Stephen, Anne Murcott and Anneke H, van Otterloo 1992: The Sociology of Food: Eating, Diet, and Culture. *Current Sociology* 40(2) 1–151.

Mizushima, Kanae 1975: *Shinshitsu Haibun ni Miru Oyako no Shinsosei.* Ochanomizu Daigaku Kasiegakubu, Daigaku-in 75-Nendo Shushi Ronbun.

Moeran, Brian 1986: Individual, Group and *Seishin*: Japan's Internal Cultural Debate. In Takie S. William P. Lebra (eds.): *Japanese Culture and Behavior.* Pp. 62–79. Honolulu: University of Hawaii Press.

Morioka, Kiyomi 1973: *Kazoku Shuki Ron.* Tokyo Baifukan.

Mulkay, Michael 1988: *On Humour: Its Nature and Its Place in Modern Society.* London: Polity.

Munn, Nancy D. 1992: The Cultural Anthropology of Time: A Critical Essay. *Annual Review of Anthropology* 21: 93–123.

Murcott, Anne 1984: Introduction. In Anne Murcott (ed.): *The Sociology of Food and Eating.* Pp. 1–5. London: Gower.

Myers, Fred R. 1988: The Logic and Meaning of Anger Among Pintupi Aborigines. *Man* 23: 589–610.

Nakane, Chie 1973: *Japanese Society.* Harmondsworth: Penguin.

Newson, John and Elizabeth 1974: Cultural Aspects of Childrearing in the English Speaking World. In M.P.M. Richards (ed.): *The Integration of a Child into a Social World.* Pp. 52–82. Cambridge: Cambridge University Press.

Nihon Fujin Dantai Rengokai 1980: *Fujin Hakusho.* Tokyo: Tokyo Seikyo.

O'Conner, Sorca 1992: Legitimating the State's Involvement in Early Childhood Programs. In Bruce Fuller and Richard Rubinson (eds.): *The Political Construction of Education: The State, School Expansion, and Economic Change.* Pp. 89–98. New York: Praeger.

Ortner, Sherry B. 1973: On Key Symbols. *American Anthropologist* 75: 1338–46.

Otsu-shi 1981: *Hoikuen ni Tsuite.* Otsu: Otsu Shiyakusho.

Peak, Lois 1989: Learning to Become Part of the Group: The Japanese Child's Transition to Preschool Life. *Journal of Japanese Studies* 15(1): 93–124.

Peak, Lois 1991a: *Learning to Go to School in Japan: The Transition from Home to Preschool Life.* Berkeley: University of California Press.

Peak, Lois 1991b: Training Learning Skills and Attitudes in Japanese Early Education Settings. In Barbara Finkelstein, Anne E. Imamura, and Joseph Tobin (eds.): *Transcending Stereotypes: Discovering Japanese Culture and Education.* Pp. 96–108. Yarmouth, Maine: Intercultural Press.

Pharr, Susan J. 1976: The Japanese Woman: Evolving Views of Life and Role. In Lewis Austin (ed.): *Japan: The Paradox of Progress.* Pp. 307–27. New Haven: Yale University Press.

Plath, David 1969: *The After Hours.* Berkeley: University of California Press.

Plath, David 1980: *Long Engagements: Maturity In Modern Japan.* Stanford: Stanford University Press.

Plath, David 1983: Introduction: Life is Just a Job Resume? In David Plath (ed.): *Work and Lifecourse in Japan.* Pp. 1–13. Albany: State University of New York Press.

Pope, Kenneth S. 1978: How Gender, Solitude, and Posture Influence the Stream of Consciousness. In Kenneth S. Pope and Jerome L. Singer (eds.): *The Stream of Consciousness.* Pp. 259–99. New York: Plenum.

Provence, Sally, Audrey Naylor and June Paterson 1977: *The Challenge of Day-Care.* New Haven: Yale University Press.

Roberts, Glenda S. 1986: *Non-Trivial Pursuits: Japanese Blue-Collar Women and the Life-Time Employment System.* Ph.D. Dissertation. Cornell University.

Robertson, Jennifer 1992: *Native and Newcomer: Making and Remaking a Japanese City.* Berkeley: University of California Press.

Robinson, Nancy M., Halbert B. Robinson, Martha A. Darling, and Gretchen Holm 1979: *A World of Children: Daycare and Preschool Institutions.* Monterey, Calif.: Brooks/Cole.

Rohlen, Thomas P. 1974: *For Harmony and Strength: Japanese White-Collar Organization in Anthropological Perspective.* Berkeley: University of California Press.

Rohlen, Thomas P. 1986: 'Spiritual Education' in a Japanese Bank. In Takie S. and William P. Lebra (eds): *Japanese Culture and Behavior.* Pp. 307–35. Honolulu: University of Hawaii Press.

Rohlen, Thomas P. 1989a: Introduction. *Journal of Japanese Studies* 15(1): 1–4.

Rohlen, Thomas P. 1989b: Order in Japanese Society: Attachment, Authority, and Routine. *Journal of Japanese Studies* 15(1): 5–40.

Rosenberger, Nancy R. 1989: Dialectic Balance in the Polar Model of Self: The Japan Case. *Ethos* 17: 88–113.

Rosenberger, Nancy R. 1992: Introduction. In Nancy Rosenberger (ed.): *Japanese Sense of Self.* Pp. 1–20. Cambridge: Cambridge University Press.

Rossi, Alice S. 1977: A Biosocial Perspective on Parenting. *Daedalus* 106(2): 1–31.

Roth, Julius A. 1963: *Timetables.* Indianapolis: Bobbs-Merrill.

Sano, Toshiyuki 1989: Methods of Social Control and Socialization in Japanese Day-Care Centers. *Journal of Japanese Studies* 15(1): 125–38.

Saso, Mary 1990: *Women in the Japanese Workplace*. London: Hilary Chapman.

Schwartz, Barry 1973: Notes on the Sociology of Sleep. In Arnold Birenbaum and Edward Sangrin (eds.): *People in Places: The Sociology of the Familiar*. Pp. 18–34. London: Nelson.

Schwartzman, Helen B. 1978: *Transformations: The Anthropology of Children's Play*. New York: Plenum.

Shields, James J. 1989: Introduction. In James J. Shields (ed.): *Japanese Schooling: Patterns of Socialization, Equality, and Political Control*. Pp. 1–7. University Park: Pennsylvania State University Press.

Shilling, Chris 1993 *The Body and Social Theory*. London: Sage.

Singleton, John 1989: *Gambaru*: A Japanese Cultural Theory of Learning. In J.J. Shields (ed.): *Japanese Schooling*. Pp. 8–15. Philadelphia: Penn State University Press.

Smith, Robert J. 1983: *Japanese Society: Tradition, Self and the Social Order*. Cambridge: Cambridge University Press.

Smith, Robert J. and Ella Lury Wiswell 1982: *The Women of Suyemura*. Chicago: Chicago University Press.

Spiro, Melford E. 1993: Is the Western Conception of the Self 'Peculiar' within the Context of World Cultures? *Ethos* 210: 107–53.

Stoller, Paul 1989: *The Taste of Ethnographic Things: The Senses in Anthropology*. Philadelphia: University of Pennsylvania Press.

Strathern, Andrew 1994: Keeping the Body in Mind. *Social Anthropology* 2(1): 43–53.

Strauss, Claudia 1992: Models and Motives. In Roy G. D'Andrade and Claudia Strauss (eds.): *Human Motives and Cultural Models*. Pp. 1–20. Cambridge: Cambridge University Press.

Symons, Michael 1994 Simmel's Gastronomic Sociology: An Overlooked Essay. *Food and Foodways* 5(4); 333–51.

Tada, Eiko 1991: Maintaining a Balance Between *Hito* ('Person') and *Kojin* ('Individual') in a Japanese Farming Community. Ph.D. Thesis, University of California, San Diego.

Tamanoi, Mariko A. 1991: Songs as Weapons: The Culture and History of *Komori* (Nursemaids) in Modern Japan. *Journal of Asian Studies* 50(4): 793–817.

Tanaka, Masako 1984: Maternal Authority in the Japanese Family. In George A. DeVos and Takao Sofue (eds.): *Religion and the Family in East Asia*. Pp. 7–36. Berkeley: University of California Press.

Tobin, Joseph 1992: Japanese Preschools and the Pedagogy of Selfhood. In Nancy R. Rosenberger (ed.): *Japanese Sense of Self*. Pp. 1–39. Cambridge: Cambridge University Press.

Tobin, Joseph J., David Y.H. Wu, and Dana H. Davidson 1989: *Preschool in Three Cultures: Japan, China, and the United States*. New Haven: Yale University Press.

Tochio, Isao 1986: The Present Status of Day Nurseries and the Tasks Confronting Them. *Child Welfare (Japan)* September: 1–10.

Toren, Christina 1993: Making History: The Significance of Childhood Cognition for a Comparative Anthropology of the Mind. *Man* 28(3): 461–78.

Turner, Bryan S. 1984: *The Body and Society: Explorations in Social Theory*. Oxford: Basil Blackwell.

Turner, Bryan S. 1992: *Regulating Bodies: Essays in Medical Sociology*. London: Routledge.

Valsiner, Jaan 1987: *Culture and the Development of Children's Action: A Cultural-Historical Theory of Developmental Psychology*. Chichester: John Wiley.

van Hoolvert, Ernest 1979: *The Japanese Working Man: What Choice? What Reward?* Tenterden, Kent: Paul Norbury.

Van Maanen, John and Gideon Kunda 1989: 'Real Feelings': Emotional Expression and Organizational Culture. *Research in Organizational Behavior*, 11: 43–103.

Vogel, Ezra F. 1963: *Japan's New Middle Class: The Salaryman and His Family in a Tokyo Suburb*. Berkeley: University of California Press.

Waksler, Frances C. 1986: Studying Children: Phenomenological Insights. *Human Studies* 9: 71–8.

White, Merry 1987: *The Japanese Educational Challenge: A Commitment to Children*. New York: The Free Press.

White, Merry and Robert A. LeVine 1986: What is an *Ii Ko* (Good Child)? In Harold Stevenson, Hiroshi Azuma and Kenji Hakuta (eds.): *Child Development and Education in Japan*. Pp. 55–62. New York: W.H. Freeman.

Whitehill, Arthur M. 1991: *Japanese Management: Tradition and Transition*. London: Routledge.

Wikan, Unni 1989: Managing the Heart to Brighten the Face and Soul: Emotions in Balinese Morality and Health Care. *American Ethnologist* 16(2): 294–312.

Wikan, Unni 1991: Toward an Experience-Near Anthropology, *Cultural Anthropology* 6(1): 285–305.

Winnicott, D.W. 1971: *Playing and Reality*. Harmondsworth: Penguin.

Yamagata, Kiyoko 1986: Fujin no Rodo to Hoiku Mondai. In Jinshichi Chikuzen *et al.* (eds.): *Hoiku Jissen e no Jido Fukushu*. Pp. 53–131. Tokyo: Mineruba Shobo.

Yin, Robert K. 1981: The Case Study Crisis: Some Answers. *Administrative Science Quarterly* 26: 58–65.

Zijderveld, Anton C. 1968 Jokes and their Relation to Social Reality. *Social Compass* 35: 86–311.

Index